Did I Ever TELL YOU?

Dr. Steve McMikle

Did I Ever TELL YOU?

Dr. Steve McMikle

Better Endings New Beginnings
~ Minneapolis ~

© 2026 Dr. Steve McMikle

PasticheAcademy.com

First Edition: 2026

Better Endings New Beginnings, solely owned and operated by Jodee Kulp, hereby assigns and extends exclusive and full ownership rights in this work to the author. This assignment includes all rights, title, and interest in and to the manuscript and all derivative works, in all formats and media now known or hereafter developed, subject only to any separate written agreements between Better Endings New Beginnings and the author.

No portion of this book may be reproduced, stored in a retrieval system, or transmitted in any form or by any means—electronic, mechanical, photocopy, recording, scanning, or other—except for brief quotations in critical reviews or articles, without the prior written permission of author Steven McMikle.

For permissions, licensing, or other rights inquiries regarding this work, contact:

Pastiche Academy, Inc
12620 Beach Blvd. Suite 3-193
Jacksonville, FL 32246

Front Cover, Pages & Graphics: Jodee Kulp

ISBN 978-1-971663-03-6 (Paperback)

Library of Congress Control Number: 2026903025

"I love the song of the mockingbird,
Bird of four hundred voices.
I love the color of jade,
And the intoxicating scent of flowers.
But most of all,
I love my Brother—Man."

— Nezahualcóyotl,
(Aztec Philosopher—King), 1470 AD

Foreword & About the Author

Commander Steve McMikle's story is one of extraordinary breadth and human depth — a life defined by adventure, service, and the pursuit of wisdom. Readers drawn to tales of real-world heroism and personal growth will find in his experiences a treasury of lessons, humor, and hope. His journey spans continents and careers, offering a vivid portrait of a man who has lived many lives with courage and conviction.

A decorated combat veteran with nearly three decades in the U.S. Navy, McMikle served in war zones from Vietnam to the Persian Gulf and Somalia, mastering the art of leadership under fire. Along the way, he became a specialist in Muslim and African cultures, acquiring working knowledge of Arabic, French, German, Greek, and Swahili—skills that helped him bridge divides in some of the world's most volatile regions.

Beyond the battlefield, McMikle's devotion to service never waned. After his military career, he turned his focus to education and mentorship, working for over a decade with Florida's Department of Children & Families and serving as a state-certified instructor and martial arts expert who has trained more than 700 students since 1977. His blend of compassion and discipline carried over into law enforcement, where he served as a deputy sheriff in Wyoming, and into the classroom as a teacher, motivational speaker, and tutor across subjects ranging from English to business and sociology.

Academically, McMikle's background is as diverse as his career. He holds degrees in history, languages, sociology, and business, with additional studies in education. This foundation fuels his work as a lifelong learner—a man equally at home discussing world diplomacy, ancient history, or character development.

From humble farm beginnings to commanding ships at sea, from combat to counseling youth, Commander McMikle's life is a testament to adaptability and purpose. His stories illuminate the strength found in curiosity, compassion, and service well rendered. Those who read his words will not simply witness a life of courage—they will, perhaps, gain a measure of that courage themselves.

I dedicate

this work to my dear friend and mentor,

Dr. Charles Travis,

who should take his own advice

and write a book like this.

Yours in His Service,

Dr. Steve McMikle, Headmaster

Pastiche Academy, Inc.

About Did I Ever Tell You?

My name is Dr. Steven McMikle, aka "Dr. Steve"; I am entering my eighth decade at the time of this writing and have been richly blessed to have experienced a life that has been unusual, strange, unbelievable, and highly unlikely. I say, without ego, that the nature, range, and features of my life are so extraordinary that my closest friends and advisors have pressed me for years to write this book. So here it is.

You might say that the "Did I Ever Tell You" section is the "handle," which will enable my readers to understand my motivations for writing my life's legacy for future generations. It is formatted to tell the tale of my early life experiences to age 35 (1945-1980). After that, it segues into my Advanced Life Skills Syllabus for adults and older children. This book is a compilation of true stories, events, lessons learned, wisdom acquired, and anecdotes from my life. It also includes the key elements of the Advanced Life Skills Syllabus, which embodies the most profound gems of wisdom, carefully selected from the works of thousands of years' worth of creative men and women up to the present day. This book encompasses an entire spectrum of facts, experiences, events, observations, and theories, which, in Dr. Travis's opinion and mine, should be preserved in the record for the benefit of future generations. "Did I Ever Tell You" serves as the autobiographical introduction of mini books within my Advanced Life Skills Syllabus. This work represents the culmination of my life's pursuits, ambitions, and dedication. Mind you, there is no theme, central message, or guiding principle in this collection. They are a basket of random shells found on the beach—with an occasional pearl or two mixed in to keep things more interesting—that my readers may find enjoyable, beneficial, or/and simply entertaining.

This introduction not only frames the journey ahead but also encapsulates the wisdom, knowledge, and invaluable lessons I have distilled from the sweep of human thought. Spanning from the moral guidance of The Instruction of Ptah-Hotep—the earliest known Western text—through to the breakthroughs of Max Planck's quantum physics, this series traverses a vast landscape of ideas and practices. Between these pillars, the curriculum draws on essential teachings, time-honored best practices, and profound insights, gathered meticulously to empower readers with tools for a fuller, more enlightened life.

So, my personal Yellow Brick Road has finally led me to confront Oz on his Green Throne. All I can say at this point is that Humbug is not on this menu, and that I hope to have prodded in my readers a renewed sense of the awesome possibilities that are open to us… at any age.

If I have managed in some small way to accomplish these things, and any more that I have yet to, it is solely because I have followed the advice of Socrates, who was possibly the first to say that *"Wonder is the beginning of Wisdom"*.

Never close your mind to learning more;

Lightning always precedes thunder.

Always keep an open door,

And start each day with a Sense of Wonder…

—*Dr. Steve*

Did I Ever Tell You About...

WHEN MY EYES WERE FIRST OPENED TO THE UNSEEN WORLD?

"The eyes are useless when the mind is blind."
— *Ancient Proverb*
(often attributed to African or Greek wisdom traditions)

My journey to this point started on a hot, sultry summer day in July 1954; I remember it as if it were yesterday. Cicadas were buzzing; dragonflies zipped back and forth over the water. An old snapping turtle brooded under a nearby half-submerged log. It was a perfect "Tom Sawyer" day. I was sitting barefoot in my denim bib overalls, on the banks of the Mississippi River, where it ran through a corner of my grandfather's farm in the Missouri Bootheel. My grandfather (whom I often called "Engine-Daddy," because he had retired from a 40-year career as a brakeman for the Cottonbelt Railroad) and I were fishing with bamboo poles and worms. He had caught several fish (destined to be our dinner) in a row, and although we were using the same worms, and our red-and white bobbers were only a few feet apart in the murky water, I had still caught nothing.

"Grandpa, how come you keep catching fish, and I haven't even had a nibble?"

"I dunno, Stevie", he replied. "Put on a fresh worm and let me watch you for a bit."

I did as I was told and plunked my rig back where it had been all morning. Minutes passed. "OK, I think I see the problem, Stevie," he said in his kindly Will-Rogers voice. "You're scaring off the fish. They know that you're there."

"Huh? You mean the fish can see me?"

"No, Stevie. But they can *feel* you."

"How do they do that?"

Engine-Daddy grinned, "All living things have an energy, a life-force that vibrates and tells the world that they're here. You keep staring at that bobber, and they can feel you wanting them to take your bait, right through that pole, and down the fishing line, wanting that bobber to bob. And they sense danger and stay away. Here, do as I say. Put on a fresh worm, put your rig back in the water, but wedge your pole between the log and that rock, and go do something else."

I did as he said, then picked up a stick and started whittling on it. Sure enough, a minute or so later, my bobber disappeared, grandpa *whooped!*, grabbed my pole, and handed it to me. There was a beautiful, shiny, pan-sized perch wriggling on the end of my line. He soon joined a half-dozen more in our basket.

"Now, what have you learned today, Stevie?" he asked as we sputtered home in our old jalopy truck. I stared straight ahead and thought. Engine-Daddy had taught me something that loomed large in my 9-year-old brain: *never engage your mouth until you put your mind in gear, that is, don't speak without thinking first.* I replied, "All living things know about each other". He stopped the truck (which could have come straight off the set of *The Real McCoys*), turned, and looked me right in the eye.

"It's very important that you remember that. The spark of life, a little piece of God's power, is in everything. It's mostly invisible, but believe me, Stevie, it's there. God put it in all of us. That makes everything alive in the image of God. We keep that spark, even after we die…and that means we never die, we change how we carry it."

I stared straight ahead, all the bumpy, dusty way back to the farm, and thought about what grandpa had said.

And I never forgot what I learned that day. "What truths about yourself or the world might you be missing because of the way you choose to see?"

For more on this topic, see Advanced Life Skills Syllabus Section VI: Mysteries: Knowing What You Don't Know.

Did I Ever Tell You About...

MY FIRST REAL KISS

*"Every heart sings a song,
incomplete, until another heart whispers back."*
— *Plato*

I was raised—during the summers, at least—on my grandpa's farm in the Bootheel of Missouri. The Mighty Mississippi ran through a corner of it, and starting when I was nine, every summer when school let out, Mom and Dad loaded me onto a Greyhound bus and shipped me to Cape Girardeau, MO, the nearest town of any size to our farm. "Cape", as the locals call it, is known for being the birthplace of Rush Limbaugh and for being the site of Southeast Missouri State Teachers' College. I didn't realize it at the time, but that was destined to be the location of my first year of college. The farm itself has a fascinating history, so let me tell you about that first...

My great-great-great-great-great-grandfather, Corporal William Brown, served in the Continental Army. Recruited out of the Colony of Virginia, Corporal Brown was an imposing man, standing over six feet tall, and had a true frontiersman's skill with musket, hatchet, and knife. He was assigned to duty as George Washington's Personal Bodyguard. As grandpa told the story, during one of the many desperate running skirmishes that characterized our Revolution, he threw himself between the General and a Redcoat who was taking aim at him at point-blank range. The official archives of the War Department indicate that my ancestor was struck by a .69 caliber Brown Bess musket ball intended for George. For this extraordinary act of courage, General Washington created the Order of the Purple Heart, America's first military decoration, to award to William and a sergeant from another company. The original award was a purple cloth heart with the words "MERIT" embroidered on it, which was sewn onto the uniform. That's why, to this day, the Purple Heart medal bears the General's silhouette.

As further recognition of his sacrifice, Corporal Brown was awarded 1,000 acres of frontier land on the banks of the Mississippi. That was how our family acquired the farm. Every adult male in our family since—on my grandpa's side—has served in our military: the War of 1812; the Mexican War; the Civil War (both sides); the Spanish-American War; WW I, WW II, Korea—and in my case, Vietnam, the Gulf War, and Somalia…plus a few other "hush-hush" operations, about which I am not at liberty to discuss.

Our farm, along with the surrounding forests, produced nearly everything we ate. We grew corn, hay, and vegetables, and had a 200-acre pear orchard. We kept cows, pigs, chickens, and ducks, and harvested fish, deer, rabbits, geese, and pheasants. We also raised and trained beagle puppies for breeding and hunting, so I have very early memories of being furiously licked all over by wiggling little balls of fur. The only things we bought in Cape or at the general store in Illmo (the nearest small town, pop. 800) were feed, seed, fertilizer, salt, baking powder, tools, etc. I learned early on how to hunt, fish, and perform the many tasks that John-Boy Walton supposedly did in the popular TV series, *The Waltons*. The pear orchard was especially lucrative. Grandma ("Mimi") made pear preserves and pickled pears.

Grandpa had a recipe for pear wine that was very popular, and was our best "cash crop". Customers lined up by the dozens—some of whom drove all the way from St. Louis, 120 miles north—to visit our roadside stand and buy "Tucker's Pear Elixir" at $1 for a gallon jug. I can't be certain, but I think grandpa added a healthy dash of his "corn squeezin's" to the mix, from our still that was hidden out back of the house. Whatever his recipe was, I know that my ears buzzed when I was first allowed to try it. My mom objected, of course, but grandpa told her, "Better that Stevie find out about booze with us, than with a bunch of strangers". Booze wasn't the only thing that I discovered on the farm. And that is the real subject of this particular story…

Pearlie May was the 15-year-old daughter of one of our farmhands. Grandpa had three Black families that lived in small bungalows, a few hundred feet behind the main house, separated by two "2-holer" outhouses (we had no indoor plumbing except for the pump in the kitchen). Grandpa was a kindly man; he not only provided room and board for his farmhands, but also paid them fair wages and even a share of the farm's profits. None of the other farmers around us did that for their workers, but as Grandpa told me, *"A man works harder when he's got some skin in the game."* It must have been true, because season after season, we harvested more yield per acre than the other farmers did.

Anyway, Pearlie May was, to my 12-year-old eyes, the most beautiful thing I had ever seen: huge brown eyes, buttery soft skin the color of coffee-and-cream, and teeth as white as pearls, hence her name. For many days, we worked shoulder to shoulder in the vegetable fields, weeding and pruning the plants as they bloomed and ripened. Her sweat smelled sweet, and she always had a faint whiff of cologne about her. I started having feelings that I didn't recognize—and somehow, Pearlie May knew. One day, we were picking blackberries and loading them into big baskets bound for the market. The day was clear and hot, so we agreed to take a water break and headed toward the pump at the edge of the field. As we shared the tin cup chained to the pump, she gave me one of her dazzling smiles and said, "You're really cute, ya know?"

For one heart-stopping moment, I just stared. "I-I am?" I stammered.

"C'mere", she said, and looking around to see if anyone was watching, she pulled me into those big bumps that showed through her T-shirt, and gave me a long, wet kiss. I felt her tongue pushing against my teeth and forcing its way into my mouth. I was in shock. My face felt blazing hot. A buzz, like I got when I drank grandpa's Pear Elixir, seized me, and my stomach felt like it did when I was going down an elevator. I didn't want it ever to stop. But Pearlie May finally pulled away and whispered, "Now, promise me you won't tell nobody what we done, or I'll get in trouble!"

"I-I-I promise", I stammered again, and stood motionless while my newly-found angel strolled toward the sorting house with her basket. I hardly slept that night.

That was not the last time that Pearlie May and I found excuses to run off together. She knew so much more than I did, and soon I was as much in love as a 12-year-old boy can be. But eventually, her family sensed what was going on, and our innocent rendezvous became less and less frequent. Then one day she looked down and said, "I can't see you no more, my mama says to keep away from you." And so it was. Her family moved away at the end of that season, and I never saw my First Love again. *But sometimes, in the stillness of the night, I still see her huge, brown eyes swimming in my dreams, and remember…*

Do you ever wonder what has become of people you encountered long ago?

For more on this topic, see Advanced Life Skills Syllabus Section V:
Rules of Success to Adopt Before Your 20's

Did I Ever Tell You About...

WHAT I LEARNED GROWING UP ON A FARM?

"Trust in the Lord with all your heart and lean not on your own understanding; in all your ways submit to Him, and He will make your paths straight."
— *Proverbs 3:5–6*

I'm truly sorry for all the young men and women who never get the chance to learn what a farmer's kid knows by the time he/she is "knee high to a grasshopper". You learn things and are exposed to experiences that city kids only learn from books. There are still children out there who really believe that milk comes from cartons. They can't help it, I guess. So, I'll tell you a little about the difference it makes. And, of course, I'll mix in a few other useful things in the process. For instance, **did you know that you can hear corn growing?** Most folks don't know that corn, along with most other leafy plants, manufactures food in the sunlight and grows only at night. We had no air conditioning, so we left our windows open at night. My upstairs bedroom bordered 200 acres of young, green corn, and in the stillness, broken only by the chirping of crickets, a sound like a giant sheet of cellophane crackling was clearly audible. This was the sound of corn growing. That, and finding out where milk actually comes from, are one of many things that farm kids learn, and that city kids probably never will.

Because my dad was a career Navy sailor, we had to move frequently. He had a specialty (amphibious warfare) that forced us to relocate every couple of years, and sometimes more frequently than that. In fact, I spent my K-12 education in over 20 different schools across 18 other states. Still, when school let out in May, it was a Greyhound bus ride to the farm until September.

The only year that this did not occur was when I was 16, and that was due to a serious surgery that Mom had, and I stayed home to take care of her while she recovered, because Dad was deployed to the Pacific.

One of the principal benefits of all these relocations was that they taught me how to adapt and overcome. I was already learning that on the farm, but changing environments sharpened that tool even more. *Farm life is unforgiving and uncompromising. There is no such thing as a "day off". You have obligations and responsibilities, and as they used to say in the old Navy days of sail, "Growl ye may, but go ye must!"*

My very first job, during my first summer there at 9 years old, was gathering eggs. We had some four dozen chickens, and one feisty old rooster that kept busy servicing the brood hens. My job began before sunup and before breakfast. Our henhouse was a long, narrow wooden building with a leaky roof and rows of hens in small stalls lined with straw. The hens were usually asleep, and I had to slip my small hands under the hen, remove the egg or eggs, and simultaneously slip a glass egg underneath. Hens sometimes pout and become depressed if their eggs are missing, and stop laying eggs due to "empty nest syndrome". Most people don't know this about hens, but they have feelings, just like people. Sometimes, they woke up and would peck furiously at my hands; I still bear scars on both hands. One morning, I walked into the kitchen with blood dripping from my sleeves.

Grandma yelled, "Land o' Goshen, Stevie! What happened?"

I looked down at my hands and said, "Oh, the hens do that, Mimi. They don't like me takin' their eggs, I guess."

Grandma ran upstairs and came back down with a pair of Grandpa's old work gloves, and her button-box, in which she kept the many items needed to perform small repairs on clothing. She sat at the table for a few minutes. "Stevie, watch the biscuits, don't let 'em burn."

"Yes, ma'am," I replied. She came to me after working her magic with grandpa's gloves. She had cut and sewn them to fit my small hands.

Milking cows was another matter. We had eight milking cows, each with a distinct personality. I learned that cows have feelings too, and that you should rub your hands together to warm them up before grabbing a teat. You can get a nasty kick from a cow that doesn't like the way you're pulling on her. One cow, in particular, was particularly sensitive; "Flower" would acknowledge my appearance with a low moooo of greeting, but would literally "kick the bucket" if I wasn't careful not to pull on her too hard. Mimi and Engine-Daddy were survivors, veterans of WW I and the Depression. Many "Kings of the Road", victims of the economic upheaval still shaking the nation after V-E Day, would knock on our door. As I mentioned earlier, Grandpa was a kind man. The presence of the Cotton Belt railroad track and roundhouse, just a half-mile or so east of the farm, assured a steady flow of visitors. He never turned a hungry man away. Often, he would feed them for a day in return for an honest day's work, like cutting a cord of firewood or digging an irrigation ditch. Mimi would patch their tattered clothes and even offer a hot bath in the big washtub under the giant oak in our backyard.

I remember one of Mimi's Words of Wisdom from the Depression: *"Use it up. Wear it out. Make it do."* One of our visitors wore what had once been an expensive business suit.

We sat and listened to his story as he shoveled down a plateful of grandma's beans and cornbread; "I used to own a beautiful dress shop in downtown Chicago. Fine ladies would come in from all over and buy the latest Paris designs. Then one day they just stopped comin'. Their husbands were all off fighting the war. I was ruined; I lost my house, my car. My wife ran off with my best friend. I've got to start over somehow." We fixed him up with a sack of food, prayed with him, and watched him out of sight as he headed down the gravel road leading to the railroad station.

Our kitchen was the largest room in the house. We had an old cast-iron stove, which burned wood or coal, and a huge table made of two-by-fours nailed to wooden sawhorses that took up most of the room. Grandma cooked breakfast for us and the farm hands, who would line up at the kitchen door to get their morning ration of scrambled eggs, ham, biscuits and gravy, cornbread, griddle-cakes, and honey from our own beehives, and other tasty delights from grandma's iron stove, which she laid out in huge, steaming platters.

In the days when many Americans performed demanding physical labor all day, a 1,000-calorie breakfast was necessary to fuel their engines. Now, our technically saturated workdays are spent in cubicles or other small, confined spaces. Yet, many still eat "traditional", fat- and protein-saturated meals, which we consequently fail to burn up. Where do you think all those unburned calories go? This is just one factor contributing to America's Obesity Epidemic. Our work day went from pre-dawn to sunset, and we didn't stop except for lunch, which we ate from dinner pails wherever on the 1,000-acre farm we were when the lunch whistle blew.

The job I dreaded most was the hay harvest, which involved walking behind our flatbed truck and lifting bales of hay onto it. They were often heavy with dew and weighed 60-70 lbs. apiece. After several hours, my back and shoulders cried out in pain. At the end of the day, Mimi would rub horse liniment on my aching muscles. By the end of the season, however, I had become accustomed to the hard work and could lift and toss a heavy bale over my head with ease.

Did I ever tell you that Engine-Daddy was a war hero? One Sunday afternoon, when we had a break from the regular workday schedule, I was rummaging through some boxes in the basement. I discovered an old steamer trunk filled with dark brown uniforms, accompanied by a scrapbook containing fascinating photos and postcards. There was Grandpa, standing at attention while some important-looking man was pinning a medal on his chest. I found out years later that the man was General George "Blackjack" Pershing, and that my grandpa was receiving the medal for being the WWI Allied Boxing Champion. At supper that evening, I asked him about the medal. "Oh, that. Yeah, Stevie, the General was real proud of the fact that our team won out over the Frogs and Tommies."

"The what?" I asked.

"The French and British soldiers. I'm a fair boxer, and managed to beat their boxers pretty quickly."

"Fair boxer", I discovered from Mimi, was a gross understatement. She showed me Engine-Daddy's scrapbook, where he was being awarded trophies and medals for his athletic prowess, going back years. Grandpa was 6'3" and carried some 230 pounds of solid muscle. His 40-year career as a railroad brakeman and his avocation as a farmer had left his huge, callused hands with a fearsome grip. We had a few pecan trees, and grandpa showed me a trick where he could take a handful of the hard shells and crush them into fragments with his bare, calloused hands.

"Why didn't you tell me, grandpa?"

He sighed and tossed another piece of wood into Grandma's iron stove. *"A man who talks about himself too much doesn't really have much to talk about".* I thought about that while the fresh wood popped and sizzled in the firebox. *"He lets what he does do the talking".* Grandpa always seemed to make perfect sense.

Among his other qualities, He was surprisingly well-read. Far from being a stereotypical redneck farmer, he could quote Shakespeare, Marcus Aurelius, and random Scriptures with ease. He applied the Pythagorean Theorem and could solve complicated calculations using a worn wood abacus. I worshipped him and never wanted some summers to end. I have an old black-and-white photo of my grandpa and me standing side by side in silhouette; except for size, our profiles were identical. He taught me to fish, shoot, and hunt with a rifle and a 20-gauge. And the summer I turned 12, he gave me what had been Mom's Sears & Roebuck bolt-action .22 cal. Rifle. From then on, whenever we needed fresh meat, I could usually bag several wild rabbits in a few hours. Have you ever eaten pan-fried rabbit with butter and garlic, accompanied by cornbread and fresh collards? HMMMM-MMMM. There's an indescribable satisfaction in eating meat or fish that you have harvested yourself. I so sympathize with city kids, who will probably never know this simple yet satisfying pleasure. Top that off with home-made peach ice cream (we made all our butter, cheese, and hand-cranked ice cream), and I swear that no millionaire ever dined better.

Grandpa also taught me how to dream productively. Night after night, we would sit in wooden chairs in the backyard, and with a cloud of fireflies flitting around us, he would point out the different constellations and explain their fascinating history. Orion was my favorite because it looked exactly as it was supposed to. With bright red Betelgeuse at his center, the Heart of the Hunter has always had an attraction for me, even before the movie came out. But more importantly, he taught me how to "picture" my dreams. What the self-improvement enthusiasts now call "proactive visualization," he called "picturing." And it's probably the single most profound thing that Engine-Daddy ever taught me.

"Imagine what you want, Stevie. I mean, the really big, important things. See them in as great a detail as you can manage. Give them color, and shape, and sound. Then, put your face right in the middle of that picture. Pray to Father God about them, and ask Him to give them to you, but only if He thinks it's the right thing for you. And then trust Him to do the right thing, even if the answer is no. Trust Him with all your heart. And he won't let you down. But you can't just sit on your backside and wait; you have to work at it with all your heart. And not just 'dabble' at it---work on them as if your life depends on it, because guess what? ---IT DOES!" Nearly seven decades later, I can still hear those precious Words of Wisdom. And I have lived every day since then, trying to follow his advice.

Another of the many things he taught me on the farm, and perhaps the most important thing of all: HONOR. The way this came about was one time we visited the general store in Illmo. We drove the jalopy flatbed into town to pick up a few sacks of seed on a sweltering morning, and after they were loaded, Grandpa came in to pay and saw me staring at the tall candy jars on the counter. I had a thing for licorice whips. Grandpa read my mind. "Go ahead, Stevie. You deserve a treat. Get yourself some'". I was paid an allowance of a dollar a week for my work, and my four quarters were still burning a hole in my pocket. Licorice whips were three for a nickel, and I could already taste their rich fragrance.

"I'll take six licorice whips, please, sir," I said to the clerk, and he put them in a paper bag and handed them over. We were about a mile down the road back when I opened the bag to savor my new delight.

"Hey, Grandpa, Mr. Edwards put in seven whips! Guess he miscounted." The truck skidded to stop, and gravel flew up in the air. Grandpa turned around and chugged back towards the store.

"Why are we going back, Grandpa? It's only worth a couple of cents, and I'm sure Mr. Edwards won't mind."

He had a grim look on his face. "It doesn't matter how much they are. It's the principle." We pulled up to the store and walked up to the counter. "Tom, Stevie has something to tell you". He looked down at me and nodded.

"Mr. Edwards, you gave me one too many licorice whips. I came back to return it." The clerk looked down at me and smiled. He and Grandpa were friends, and they traded a grin and a wink.

"Well, that's very honest of you, young man.. But since I can't make change for less than a penny, you may as well keep it. But thanks for coming back."

I was silent for the first mile or two. Then Grandpa said, "Stevie, tell me, what do you think just happened back there?" I knew that this was one of his "think about it" questions, so I thought carefully before putting my tongue in gear.

"It would have been wrong to keep the extra piece without paying for it, right?"

"That's right. But do you know why it would have been wrong?"

I knew now that this was one of those questions, so I sat and thought about it. "It would have been wrong to take it, right?"

"Yes, but why would it have been wrong? Think, Stevie. Why?" This time he didn't wait for me to speak; this was what I would learn, in later years, something called a "rhetorical question". *"Because, my fine little man, it would have been dishonorable."*

Over the next few days, Engine-Daddy taught me all he knew about honor; what it was; how you have to earn it; how precious it is to have; how difficult it is to keep; how terrible it is to lose.

This was probably one of the most important things that I learned that whole summer.

*"How would your dreams and goals change if you trusted God
not just with the outcome, but with the journey,
and committed to working toward them wholeheartedly
—even if God's answer is different from what you expect?"*

*For more on this topic, see Advanced Life Skills Syllabus Section I:
Effective Human Communications*

Did I Ever Tell You About...

WHAT IT'S LIKE TO BE HOME-SCHOOLED?

*"It is better to fight and fall
than to live without hope."*
— *Viking Proverb, The Saga of the Volsungs*

When I turned 5 years old, we were living in Fall River, Massachusetts, a town near Boston. My Dad had been assigned duty on a Navy destroyer home-ported in Boston, and he spent most of his time at sea. I remember Fall River as being full of aging red-brick buildings that all looked as if they were over a hundred years old, and that the people spoke with a strange accent that I didn't recognize. The part of Fall River we lived in had a heavy Portuguese-speaking population. They ate things like periwinkles, which they scraped off rocks at the beach, and then dug out of their shells with safety pins, and served in melted butter. The locals called the city "Bah-stin", and pronounced everything differently than I had ever heard. They drank "coa-fee", "pahked "their cahs, and their dogs bahked in the yahd.

My manner of speech was strange to them, as well. Anyway, this was about the time I discovered what Mom called my special gift: I could memorize things without even trying. We had moved to Fall River from the farm the previous summer, just before school started. Mom had been home-schooling me ever since I learned to talk. She began with "picture books", from which I quickly learned to read. Before I knew it, I was also writing, starting with printing block letters, then cursive. I discovered that I could remember things I had read the day before without going back to the book. I didn't think it was anything special, but my Mom seemed surprised that I could quote back stories she had read to me a few days before. She kept coming home from the library with new books, and I read through them in just a few days time. She started having me write book reports on what I had I learned. By the time I started kindergarten that fall, I could already read and write when I walked into the classroom door. The teachers were perplexed, and didn't know what to make of me. Back at home I started reading poetry, and my mom was astounded when I could stand and recite the first dozen or so stanzas of Longfellow's "Song of Hiawatha" from memory. I remember her inviting the other Navy wives in the neighborhood over for tea, to hear me recite:

"By the shores of Gitchee-Gumee, by the shining Big-Sea Water, stood the wigwam of Nokomis, Daughter of the Moon, Nokomis. Dark behind it rose the forest, rose the dark and gloomy pine-trees, rose the firs with cones upon them. Bright before it beat the water, beat the clear and sunny water, beat the shining Big-Sea water"… and on and on for dozens of stanzas more. I could do likewise with some of Shakespeare's works. My favorite was Macbeth's Act V soliloquy, which is still a favorite to this day.

My Mom talked Dad into buying a set of encyclopedias, which I avidly devoured from A to Z over the next few years. I remember my grade-school principal, Mrs. Lenahan, calling my mom and me into a conference in her office.

Schools in those days did not have "gifted" programs, so Mrs. Lenahan, who took a great liking to me, started giving me extra-credit assignments far above my grade level. I completed these with relish. By the time I reached third grade, my teachers were allowing me to teach lessons in class about select topics; "dinosaurs" was one of my favorites, but I also recall teaching lessons in the general sciences, other cultures, and history. I had started reading the works of authors like Jules Verne and Charles Dickens. Mrs. Lenahan would sometimes come and listen from the back of the classroom. And thus, I discovered a flaw in my character: *hubris*. I enjoyed the extra attention and approval I was getting so much that I found myself craving it, and doing what was necessary to get more. This became a dangerous addiction, and I struggled with it for years. The bottom line was that I skipped over fourth grade entirely, and had just started fifth grade when Dad was transferred to a ship based in Charleston, SC. And that first day of school brought a form of "culture shock" to my naïve young world. It was an absolute wake-up call.

"What's in the bag, kid?" I looked up from where I was sitting under a tree at the edge of the playground. It was lunch break; I had been enrolled into Jefferson Davis Elementary School in Charleston for the fall semester of fifth grade. The first thing I had noticed was that everyone in my class was bigger than me. I've always been short, but a year's age difference amplified my lack of stature. The person standing over me was a tall, gangly red-head whose name, I later found out, was Andy. He was the school bully. He and two of his cronies were standing there looking down at me.

"My lunch", I replied to his question.

"Give it over, let's see what you've got to trade."

"Trade for what?", I asked.

"For me not beating you up", was his grinning, gap-toothed reply. His comrades chuckled in anticipation...

Very early on the farm, Grandpa had taught me the basics of self-defense. I was also very strong for my age, and I have pictures of myself chinning myself at the age of eight months and walking on my hands at three. So, I stood up and said to Andy, "I'm not giving you my lunch". When he reached to push me, I kicked him squarely where Grandpa had taught me to, hard enough to make him fall and roll on the ground, groaning in pain. His two buddies jumped on me, and punched and kicked me repeatedly. I sustained a split lip, two black eyes, and a bloody nose. But Andy had to be dragged off by both of them, still groaning. So much for my first day of school. That was the last time anyone bothered me at that school. Andy ended up being a friend and companion. I helped the three of them with their homework, and from that time on, I was their hero. My nickname at school was "The Brain." The teachers at Jeff Davis had a different reaction from the ones in Fall River; I was a "special case" student. They mainly steered clear of me as long as I turned everything in on time. I scored consistent "A"s in all subjects. I wouldn't ask many questions in class, because I often felt as if I understood the subject being taught as well as, or even better than, the teachers did themselves.

I moved a total of twenty times during my childhood, and from kindergarten to 12th grade, I attended a grand total of 18 different schools, spanning Boston, Texas, California, and the in-between areas. But it was at Long Beach Polytechnic High School, at the wise old age of fifteen, that l discovered my true gift: languages. I had studied enough to decide that I wanted to be an archaeologist, someone who traveled the world and discovered mummies and other ancient things; in other words, I wanted to be Indiana Jones, long before Harrison Ford was even born. Archaeologists needed to be skilled in ancient languages, so I started teaching myself Latin, then Greek, and, because it was the *lingua franca* in much of what was once the "ancient world," Arabic.

By the time I turned sixteen, I could speak, read, and write fairly well in all three tongues. I eventually discarded the idea of being another Indiana Jones, when I discovered years later that, far from discovering gold statues in some hidden ancient tomb, real field archaeology consisted mainly of hours and hours on one's knees, picking potsherds and other tiny remnants of ancient civilizations, out of the sand and rock; and being paid little or nothing for that back-breaking work. Furthermore, unless one taught archaeology for a living, became a museum curator, or received a rare grant from National Geographic, there was little to no money to be made in the profession. But by the time I discovered this unpleasant reality, I had become quite comfortable with Middle Kingdom Egyptian hieroglyph, Sumerian and Babylonian cuneiform, Phoenician, Aramaic, and several other ancient languages. Not until many years later, when I was a Navy Commander serving on General Norman Schwartzkopf's personal staff as his Arabic go-to guy, did I finally fulfill the dream of a lifetime and get to visit the ruins of ancient Babylon, restored by the Iraqis as a national landmark. The General, who had become a trusted acquaintance during the Gulf War, was aware of my childhood passion and offered me a Humvee and a driver for the day, allowing me to visit Babylon and make rubbings of some of the magnificent bas-relief carvings there. For me, it was a lifelong dream, finally fulfilled.

When I was finishing up my junior year at San Diego High School, My Dad retired from the Navy after 20 years of service. He quit then, we learned, because —in his words—the Navy was becoming too "sissified" for him to stay. There was a new Admiral, by the name of Zumwalt, who was eliminating many of the old Navy traditions that Dad so loved. So, despite the Navy's best efforts to dissuade him, he got out. We moved to Jacksonville, FL that Spring, where I was destined to complete my Senior year at Robert E. Lee High School. He relocated there because, as Mom later told me, it was right on the ocean, there were three Navy bases, good weather year-round, and some of the best fishing anywhere. And so, the McMikle family picked up and moved again, this time for good.

For more on this topic, see Advanced Life Skills Syllabus Section II:
Put on Your Full Armour for the Arena

Did I Ever Tell You About...

THE PROCESS OF TRANSFORMING FROM BOYHOOD TO MANHOOD?

*"Every heart sings a song,
incomplete, until another heart whispers back."*
— Plato

One of the many things I had sacrificed during this unusual childhood journey was a social life —and social skills in general. When you move as many times as I did growing up, you don't get to form lasting friendships; you aren't in one place long enough to develop any real social skills, and your memories are only to be found in a yearbook. Other than with Pearlie May, I had never kissed a girl, dated, or formed any lasting bonds with anyone outside of my Mom and Dad. They were not a very physically expressive couple, and I knew no better. I did not even have a driver's license. This was my Mom's idea of keeping me from being "tempted"; she was an extremely religious person who believed that sex was for married couples only, so any social life was strongly discouraged. By the time my Senior year at Robert E. Lee High School was drawing to a close, I was still, for the most part, a social nobody. I had carried a solid 4.0+ GPA, was a member of the National Honor Society, and had received several scholastic awards from local groups, including the Lions Club and Rotary. All my energies, in my young life, I devoted to learning. One of the payoffs—or so I thought—was to be my Class Valedictorian—and I looked forward to this honor with great anticipation.

One day, the principal called my Mom and me in to meet with him. He was an overweight, pale, sweaty man. He "harumphed" after sitting down behind his massive desk. "No one knows your boy, Mrs. McMikle", he began. "Now, according to the grade scores, Steven is far and away the best student in the school. But if he gets up to deliver the Valedictorian address, most of the people he goes to school with won't recognize him up there. So, we're requesting that you stand aside and allow Mary Ann Simmons to speak as Valedictorian".

Mary Ann was the daughter of the owner of the local Oldsmobile dealership, and he donated the funds to buy the Generals, our championship football team, all their uniforms and equipment. She only had a B average at best, but politics is what it is. This was my first encounter with good-ole-boy Southern traditions. You went along to get along, and so it was that I sat silently in the audience, waiting to walk up onstage and receive my diploma like everyone else. Mary Ann Simmons spoke haltingly about how the Class of '63 was going to make the world a better place.

My Senior Prom was where the other part of my education—the one involving females—was about to begin. Linda was in the school chess club, as I was. She lived with her Mom, only a few blocks from our house, so we started hanging out at each other's homes to play chess and drink iced tea. Linda was taller and two years older than I, having been held back twice due to poor grades. She was not only much more experienced in the ways of the world than I, but she also had a part-time job and owned her own car—a beat-up 1957 Ford Fairlane.

I started helping her with her homework, and she started to show me her appreciation in the most wonderful ways. Linda taught me how to kiss, and how to "pet", and we used to play footsie under the chess table for hours at a time. The reason remained a mystery to me until very recently, but taller women have always been attracted to me. And Linda was a very tall, buxom brunette, with full, red lips that begged to be kissed. So, although I hadn't thought of going, she asked to be my date for the Senior Prom. You couldn't say that we loved each other, but we both liked each other a lot, and that was enough. Like the song says, "I used her, and she used me, but neither one cared, we were getting' our share." The night of the Senior Prom, held at the Sea Turtle restaurant and ballroom right on the beach, is burned forever into my memory. After the dance, we found a secluded sand dune, and there, on an old blanket that she had in the trunk, Linda took my virginity. She knew that this was my first time, and Linda showed me a gentle, almost maternal side of herself as she whispered to me what to do. The Genie was out of the Bottle… and I was never the same.

All that Summer, I prepared for the next great adventure: college. My parents had saved enough to not only pay cash for our home but also to fund my first two semesters at Southeast Missouri State College—"SEMO," located in Cape Girardeau, MO. My graduation present from Mom and Dad was a bright red, two-stroke Allstate Compact scooter, which was to be my personal transportation for the next year or so. I got a room in Cheney Hall Men's Dormitory on campus, and thus entered the World of Academia…and Sex Ed 101, with the dazzling array of beautiful young co-eds that populated the campus. I loaded up my first-semester curriculum with subjects I was interested in: German, French, Biology, World History, etc. I started with stars in my eyes and a genuine desire to learn, but then I discovered the "Greek Life"—fraternities and sororities, or I should say, it found me.

With my innocent, naïve, "John Boy" self, I was truly a tempting target for the fraternity system. There were several prominent fraternities and sororities on campus for young men. The top of the food chain was Sigma Chi; then came Pi Kappa Alpha, Sigma Alpha Epsilon, and the infamous "TEKE'S"—Tau Kappa Epsilon. These were the "Animal House" guys on campus, and rumors about their wild, sex-and booze-filled marathon parties were all the buzz on campus. I didn't know that the frats had a grade point average competition on campus. Each year, the fraternity and sorority with the highest GPA average were awarded the coveted Dean's Scholarship Trophy and received multiple other perks from the Administration. I was "rushed" by several frats because my perfect GPA would significantly boost the score of whatever frat successfully recruited me. The "Sigs"— Sigma Chi—wanted me badly, but their dues were sky-high beyond my meager budget; hence their nickname on campus as "The Rich Bastards". I finally succumbed to the "Pikes"—Pi Kappa Alpha—and remain a member to this day. With my part-time job at the college library, I could easily afford their dues. Besides, a very pretty member of their sister sorority, the Tri-Delts (Delta Delta Delta) "rushed" me so persuasively that I couldn't refuse.

My first fraternity party was one of those life-altering events that become permanently etched into memory. It was held on the farm owned by the family of Frank's brother; he also happened to be the Rush Chairman and Pledgemaster, and it was his baby sister—Sandy—who was the persuasive TriDelt who had convinced me to join. We sat on hay bales laid out around a roaring bonfire in front of their barn. In the center was a large, zinc washtub full of grape Kool-Aid, and into the tub was poured whatever forms of alcohol were available to us: vodka, gin, bourbon, rum, wine, and even a splash of corn squeezin's from Frank's father's still. This potent mixture was dubbed "Purple Jesus." When I asked about the origin of the name, everyone smiled and assured me that I would find out, and so

I did. I dipped my cup into the mix, took a long swallow, gasped, and exclaimed "JEEEESUS!" And so, my question was answered. The flames obscured the other couples gathered at the edge of the fire, but I could tell that the Purple Jesus was having a similar effect on them. The last thing I remember that night was Sandy, pulling me back into the shadows of the barn, kissing and moaning in my ear as she slid her cool, manicured hand down the front of my jeans…

I opened my eyes to a brilliant sunrise, shining painfully into the window of an unfamiliar bedroom. I was lying fully clothed on a four-poster bed, draped in lilac and pink. There were "girly" things everywhere, so I quickly deduced that I was not in my dorm room. I started to lift my head and was stopped by the awful, throbbing pain behind my eyes. My ears rang, and I moaned as I searched for a bathroom where there was none. Racing against my convulsing stomach, I gagged, threw open the window, and discharged about a quart of vile, stinking liquid onto the ground below. "Oh, Gaaawd!", I croaked, and this time it was a fervent prayer for relief from my misery. I was experiencing my first hangover. It took me a while to pull myself together and find my scooter in the back of Frank's pickup. He was sitting on the front porch with a cup of coffee.

"Well, our pledge scholar is awake!" It took me a moment to realize he was talking about me. "How are you feeling, Pledge McMikle?"

"Like the Trojan Army just marched through my mouth", I replied.

He chuckled and pointed to my scooter. "I'll help you get your ride down. You'd better get back to your dorm and clean up, there's a Pledge Orientation at 2 pm, and you don't want to be late or you'll get demerits".

It was a Saturday, around 11:00 am. I glanced at my watch, which had pieces of straw lodged under the wristband. I could only imagine how they got there. "Sandy really likes you, Pledge, but if you disrespect my sister, you'll get more than demerits; I will take you apart." he warned solemnly.

"Yes sir, I'll be there". I jumped on my scooter and, looking around to get my bearings, I took off for my dorm to pull myself together for the meeting.

Every Pike pledge at SEMO State got a pledge name by which he was known until he was initiated as a full Brother. Mine was "Boy Scout"; I could easily figure out why. For the rest of the school year, I was always the designated driver —the guy who had maybe two drinks and then switched to ginger ale. I was also the one who came around the next morning with aspirin and tomato juice for the other brothers, who routinely "let it all hang out". But I didn't mind my name, nor what it implied. I was, after all, a Boy Scout, and a darned good one. My merit badges were so many that I had trouble fitting them all on my bandolier. To this day, I pride myself on waking up to New Year's Day sunrise with a clear head, a clean conscience, and a positive attitude. Boy Scout, indeed—and proud of it.

On this occasion, however, I had a murky memory of Sandy, doing things to me that I'm sure must have been every young man's dream, but try as I might, I could not remember any details. The Purple Jesus had obliterated my senses. Oh, well, I was soon to be reminded. At the Pledge Orientation, we stood at attention and stared straight ahead. In contrast, the Pledgemaster (Frank) stood before each of us in turn, and berated each Pledge with equal contempt, and I suddenly had an incredible flashback …

…to the weekend that I had turned 12 years old, long ago and far away…

"STAND AT ATTENTION, BOOT! SHUT UP, LOOK STRAIGHT AHEAD, AND DO EXACTLY WHAT I TELL YOU!".

I was standing in my small room, in our Navy Housing Project apartment in Norfolk, Virginia. I had just turned twelve the day before, and I was about to receive my birthday presents officially. My dad, who was wearing his Navy Tropical White Dress uniform even though it was a Saturday and he was off-duty, was staring at me eye-to-eye with a stern expression on his face.

"You will not speak unless spoken to! You will follow my instructions to the letter. And you will move only when I tell you to move. Do you understand me, Boot?"

"Y-Yes sir". I stammered. It was my first day of orientation to what my dad called 'becoming a man.' I was confused and more than a little hurt. I had not seen this side of my father ever before, and didn't quite know what to make of it.

The night before, when he had gotten off his ship tied up at the base, he hugged Mom at the door and winked at me. "Happy Birthday, Stevie! Your birthday presents from your Mom and me won't arrive until tomorrow morning, but I promise it'll be worth the wait, and it'll be a big surprise."

"Ok, Pop! Thank you, I love you."

"We love you, too, Stevie. Now, go help Mom with supper. We've got birthday cake and ice cream for dessert."

"Yes sir,", I responded.

So, there I stood the next morning, receiving my 12th birthday present, which had arrived on a flatbed truck an hour earlier. It was in my room. It consisted of a regulation Navy Haze Gray steel upright locker and a regulation Navy Haze Gray steel bed frame, complete with a rolled-up regulation US Navy mattress and a gray blanket.

"Now, attention to orders, Boot. Before you go anywhere today, you will first install your gear in this locker and make up this rack. I want the corners of your t-shirts folded to line up, and your bed properly made." He spent the next hour patiently showing me exactly how my clothes were to be folded and stored, and how to make my bed tight, with a six-inch fold on the top sheet, and all the other things he expected of me to be "squared away". If my dad were not away at sea or on the ship, each Saturday morning from that day on, at precisely 0800, I was to stand at attention while he inspected my room. And if anything was not clean and dust-free, and every stitch of clothing I owned was not properly folded or hung, I would not only stay until that discrepancy was remedied, but also do 25 push-ups for each infraction. And so went my "Introduction to Manhood". In the weeks and months to come, I found myself wanting my father to be away at sea, or to stay on the ship, because Mom didn't expect any of this from me, and even let me sleep in before going out to play with my friends, and do what "regular" kids did on Saturdays. She still wanted me to keep my room in order and follow my dad's standards; she didn't make me stand inspection like he did, and sometimes I would go out without cleaning everything up first. But those days were relatively few, and so I developed the habits that have shaped my life to this very day—which is why, almost exactly six years later, Frank's little tirade didn't faze me one bit. In fact, I grinned a little. Frank rushed over and stuck his face in mine. "Do you think I'm funny, Pledge Boy Scout? Do you think I'm joking around here?"

"No, sir", I replied. And he continued to berate us, little knowing that I considered him a rank amateur compared to what I was used to.

I had started the school year with a perfect 4.0 GPA and managed to keep it, right up until finals week. However, college life had an unexpected twist: beautiful young co-eds, many from St. Louis with its big-city ways, were in great abundance. They became a temptation to which I had absolutely no resistance, and that ultimately led to my academic downfall. Sandy had quickly become bored with my Boy Scout-like ways and lack of experience and had moved on. But there were so many other gorgeous Tri-Deltas, and girls with no sorority affiliation ("Independents"), that my head was spinning. I learned later that the female-male ratio at SEMO State was approximately 60/40; in other words, it was what I came to call, in my Navy years, a "target-rich environment." And my Boy Scout persona provided, for some reason unbeknownst to me, an irresistible attraction for them. Word had also spread that I was a "walking encyclopedia" of sorts, and the coy and breathy requests for assistance preparing for finals, from several beautiful young co-eds, were a temptation to which I easily succumbed.

The result was that, while I helped several girls improve their grades, my average dropped a full letter grade—literally overnight. When the semester grades were posted, I was called into a meeting with my frat council and taken to task. I gave my word to remedy the problem, and so I finally became a full-fledged Pi Kappa Alpha brother, complete with garnet-and-gold pin. I buckled down and restricted my dating, and so ended the Spring semester with a GPA of 3.8, which was good enough to keep me in good graces with all concerned. It was also during that Spring semester that I discovered my entrepreneurial talent.

I knew little about "business," other than finding ways to do odd jobs to earn money. I had always been relatively good at that. Starting with Dad's two-year tour at the Kingsville, Texas, Auxiliary Naval Air Station (a bombing range for the Pensacola jet jockeys), I began to get creative. I had been receiving one dollar per week from my dad for doing my regular weekly chores: washing the supper dishes, mowing the lawn, taking out the trash, and washing the family car once a week. A dollar went a long way back then; Saturday paydays meant matinee marathons at the Texas Theater, with orange soda and popcorn, from which I still had 20 cents left over. It was still the 50s, and a little money went a long way. This was scrupulously saved in a mason jar under my rack.

I remember vividly one incredible afternoon, walking home from school, when I found myself staring breathlessly at a ten-dollar bill lying in the gutter. It was a fortune! I felt strangely guilty as I bent to grab it before the wind took it away. I was trembling with excitement, and as I looked around to see if anyone was running to retrieve it, I quickly stuffed it into my pocket. Once home, I ran to my room, closed the door, and knelt by my bunk to unfold my treasure and stare at Thomas Jefferson's face: IT WAS REAL! Still in a boyish state of shock, I took it to my writing table (which was assembled from painted orange crates), spread it out, took a pad of notebook paper, and drew up a plan. So much for this, for that…and for the rest of that month, I was King of the World. Eventually, I saved $5 and gleefully squandered the rest, but the feeling of having EXTRA MONEY OF MY OWN was something that I liked very much, so I set about thinking of ways to earn more.

 Kingsville was not a wealthy town. With a population of 27,000, it is situated 120 miles southeast of San Antonio and is located in the heart of the famous King Ranch. It was a hot, dry, dusty, tarantula-infested Cowtown. The only real enterprise going was the Naval Auxiliary Naval Station, home to 900 sailors, including my dad, who had just been promoted to Chief Quartermaster. One of my classmates was Dickie Kleberg, who was the heir to the King Ranch fortune. The county was named for his family. He rode to school in a limousine, and the staff of Lamar Elementary School was terrified of him. Dickie came to school wearing a dapper straw hat, sunglasses, and black clothing.

Why his parents didn't send him away to some expensive private academy for the Sons of the Super-Rich, I don't know to this day. He didn't need to turn in homework; it was understood by all that he was to get only A's. To me, Dickie was just a regular kid like the rest of us, and I didn't know any better at the time. Anyway, money was tight for the average family in Kingsville, but I still managed to earn a little extra. I went door-to-door, offering to wash windows and cars, mow lawns with a hand mower, and do other odd jobs, and saved up my money. People liked my work because I always did a little more than was expected. It was the memory of that time that led me, during my Spring semester at SEMO State, to open a business. The farm was only 8 miles away, and Grandma and Grandpa were more than willing to help me. I used my savings to buy a large ice chest, which I kept stocked with sodas, candy bars, crackers, cookies, and a variety of fruits from the farm. These, I resold to my fellow dorm residents at a 30% mark-up. My grandparents gave me fruit, veggies, and preserved goodies for free, so that was pure profit. There was no store nearby, and the vending machines charged a small fortune for really stale and awful snacks, so students lined up at my door during late-night study sessions to purchase my wares. I was doing well financially, and soon my savings climbed to the unheard-of sum of $300.

Then, one day during the Spring semester, I came back early on a Sunday from my weekend on the farm, unlocked my dorm room, and discovered several boys sitting on the floor, talking and laughing. It was my roommate, Dave, and his buddies. And they were eating my supplies out of the cooler. "Ooops, McMikle! You're not supposed to be back until tomorrow morning. Oh, well. We got hungry and thought you wouldn't mind if we had a snack and paid you later."

I stood with my mouth open, trying to absorb the scene. Snack? Those boys had devoured everything in my cooler except a few brownish pears from the farm. "WHAT THE HECK DO YOU THINK YOU'RE DOING, DAVE? I ASKED YOU NEVER TO GO THROUGH MY STOCK UNLESS I WAS HERE!" I was livid with rage, seeing my private things being pawed through by strangers.

"Well, we were hungry, and you weren't here. So, too bad. And if you're gonna make such a stink about it, we won't pay you at all. How do you like that, A-hole?" Dave sneered. He was a tall, lanky, street-smart kid from St. Louis. We had never gotten along and had pretty much avoided each other, except for his occasional purchases from my cooler. His three companions, who were cut from the same cloth, all stood up and formed a semi-circle around me. Dave got up and stood directly in front of me, and looked down at me from his towering 6-feet+ height. "So, what are you gonna do about it, you little jerk?", he said, as he poked his long finger into my chest.

The blind rage of righteous indignation poured over me like hot water; I literally saw red, and there was a buzzing in my ears that rose to a thunderous roar. Without even thinking, I butted Dave in his stomach, lifted him off the floor by his hips, and slammed his body into the wall. He let out a startled *whoosh!* of air as I straight-punched him hard, squarely in the solar plexus, like Grandpa had taught me. Dave turned bright pink and started choking and gasping for air. All those years of lifting hay bales over my head and performing the many other labors of life on the farm had given me a set of powerful upper-body muscles, which were obscured by my short stature. The companion who had stood next to Dave stepped toward me with his fists up. I went down into the Crouching Tiger stance that I had learned during months of judo classes at the YMCA in Jacksonville, and when he moved to strike, I grabbed his arm and threw him over my hip with practiced ease, and heard something go crack! as he hit the linoleum floor. He screamed in pain, and as I turned to face the remaining two thieves, they ran down the stairs to the echoes of their yelled defiance. The next morning, I requested, and received, a change of roommates. Word spread about the incident, and to my surprise, I had several inquiries from other young men, asking if I would teach them my "tricks". As it turned out, this marked the beginning of a long affiliation with the martial arts, which eventually became a much more lucrative source of extra income than selling snacks from a cooler. And so, I was to learn next about the poisonous thing called "prejudice". My new roommate was a youth my age, named Jack Levine; otherwise known, so I was told by my fraternity brothers, as "Jack the Jew."

*When have you chosen to fight
instead of walk away. Why?*

*For more on this topic, see Advanced Life Skills Syllabus Section V:
Rules of Success to Adopt Before Your 20's*

Did I Ever Tell You About...

WHY BIRDS OF A FEATHER FLOCK TOGETHER??

"In the sweetness of friendship let there be laughter, and the sharing of pleasures. For in the dew of little things the heart finds its morning, and is refreshed."
—Khalil Gibran, 1922

Jack Levine and I were instantly very comfortable with each other, which surprised me. My altercation with Dave had ended with his expulsion from SEMO, which was probably inevitable for him anyway, since he was on the verge of flunking out when we had our disagreement. That story had become a local legend, and suddenly my status as "Boy Scout" with the Pikes was replaced with the moniker "Odd-job". The James Bond movie "Goldfinger" had just come out, and "Odd-job" was the name of the tuxedo-wearing, Japanese sumo-warrior character that displayed skills similar to those I had used with Dave and his buddies.

Jack was a serious student whose intended major was Business. He wore black business suits all the time, and I remember that he had such a thick, dark beard that he had to shave twice as often as I. He was a natural scholar, like me.

We shared a love of history, literature, and poetry, and would spend hours discussing topics such as Thoreau's philosophy of solitude versus Emerson's naturalism. I had found a kindred spirit, someone who deeply respected learning and used the wisdom thus gained in everyday life. Jack became my friend, which is why I was so dumbfounded when I heard that I was supposed to avoid him.

"He's a Jew, a kike, a Christ-Killer, Brother McMikle. He's not like us. You shouldn't even be talking to him, let alone be roommates with him!"

Although not part of the fraternity's charter, there was an unspoken rule that non-Christians were to be avoided.

I asked Jack if he knew why.

He sighed and looked down as he took off his glasses and wiped them on his tie. "Steve, buddy—I'm used to it. It's not you're fault, you're a mensch. But to my people, you're a gentile, a non-believer. I'm not supposed to be hanging around with you, either. It's all a little stupid, if you ask me."

We talked for hours, long into the night. His grandparents were survivors of something called the Holocaust, one of the most horrendous events in all of human history. I had read about it, of course, but Jack's retelling of his grandparents' stories brought it all into a different perspective.

"Man's inhumanity to man," and everyone kept saying that we should never forget, and yadda-yadda-yadda. Yet, I saw clearly that the seeds of that same unspeakable evil were present in the attitudes displayed by my own fraternity brothers, and others whom I knew—even my grandpa and grandma!

This came as quite a shock to my naive young sensibilities. Jack saw how it affected me, something which drew us even closer as friends and roommates. In the terminology adopted in later years, Jack and I were first-class "nerds". We were like bookends: two different people with very different backgrounds, yet our similarities were very strong.

I lost track of Jack Levine after that Spring, but I still remember our shared affinity for doing things right and in accordance with rules set down by a higher power. And *I will be forever grateful to him for setting my feet on the path that ultimately compelled me to judge other people by what they individually believed and practiced, and not by what society said I should believe about them.*

Have you ever been called a 'racist'?
What do you think this term really means?

For more on this topic, see: Advanced Life Skills Syllabus Section IV:
Universal Laws, Hiding in Plain Sight

Did I Ever Tell You About...

WHAT I LEARNED ON MY JOURNEY THROUGH COLLEGE?

"Money grows on the tree of persistence."
—Japanese Proverb

The money had run out, and so I set about finding ways to continue my education. I had returned to Jacksonville, having successfully survived my first year of college with a solid 3.8 GPA, despite the siren calls of my dalliances with the fairer sex. My family was not wealthy; the military had been Dad's mother for 20 years, but now we were all at a crossroads, where, to use Engine-Daddy's words, we had to "fish or cut bait." Dad had paid $10,000 cash for our modest home in Riverside, a historic, gentrified suburb of Jacksonville, Florida. His first civilian job was Assistant Service Manager at the local Volkswagen dealership. Because, for years, the family car had been a vintage 1956 VW with a diminutive 36-hp motor, Dad had become a very skilled, self-taught VW mechanic. The money he earned sustained us, but there wasn't enough after paying the bills for me to continue my schooling.

My scooter had been wrecked while I was carrying Linda (with whom I had

had a happy reunion upon my return from SEMO). She had needed a ride to her office, where she worked as a bookkeeper. While driving at a mere 25 mph down a quiet, tree-lined street, an elderly woman driving a white Dodge ran the stop sign we were approaching. I quickly veered the scooter up and onto the curb, which flipped the scooter onto my leg, and then Linda was thrown squarely into a tree. The car stopped and backed up. I remember, to this very day, that woman's face as she stared down, open-mouthed, at our crumpled, bleeding figures on the grass, just before she gunned her engine and sped away. In my angry adrenaline rush, I got up and ran after her car, shouting at her to come back. Coming to my senses, I ran back to poor Linda, who lay moaning at the base of the tree. Her humerus was exposed, and sticking through the skin of her upper right arm; she was also bleeding from multiple cuts and abrasions, and so was I. My years of Boy Scout training instantly kicked in; I sat Linda under the tree, ripped off my shirt, and fashioned a sling for her arm. Then, I pulled my First Aid kit from the scooter's storage compartment and tended to the worst of her wounds. People had started running from their homes to assist; I asked the first to arrive to call an ambulance, which Linda and I rode to the emergency room.

Because my judo classes had trained me how to fall, I had rolled on impact, and so my own injuries were limited to cuts and scrapes, and a nasty scar where the scooter's hot tail-pipe had fallen on my thigh and branded a six-inch mark, traces of which are there to this day. Linda had sustained a cleanly broken arm and multiple gashes. Because it was her right arm, and she was right-handed, this marked the end of her employment as a bookkeeper, at least for a while. But she also qualified for unemployment insurance, which sustained her for that time. She was fitted with a ponderous cast, which in the hot Jacksonville summer was an itchy inconvenience. Over the following weeks, although I visited her as often as I could, we both knew somehow that this incident marked the end of our relationship. Although she kept insisting that she knew it wasn't my fault, I knew that she blamed me for the accident; and so it was that Linda drifted away, out of my life forever. But for me, she will always occupy that very secret, special place in every man's heart that is reserved for his "first time" girl.

Jacksonville is home to Jacksonville University, a fully-accredited, respectable school on the banks of the picturesque St. John's River. I had determined to get my bachelor's degree in Ancient History, since at that time I still entertained dreams of being an archaeologist, and that subject area seemed to be as good as any with which to begin. Tuition costs were charged by semester; for $300, I could register for as many as 18 hours (six classes @ 3 hours each. But first, I had to find a job. I saw an advertisement for a company called Sanford-Hall Office Supply for a delivery person and general "helper" around the store. They were located on Riverside Avenue, about two miles from our house. Since my scooter had been totaled, and I could not yet afford a car, Dad bought me a used bike for $10, which sum I promised to repay. When I first saw it, I was appalled to see that it was a girl's bike, and PINK!

"No worries," Pop said. He welded a steel pipe where there was supposed to be one on a boy's bike, re-painted the whole thing dark blue, and fitted it with new tires and a banana-seat, like boy's bikes had. I pedaled proudly down to Riverside Avenue and applied for the job. Mr. Sanford was a portly, cigar-smoking man in his sixties, who took an instant liking to me. I had shown up with a fresh haircut, pressed shirt and tie, a sharp, military-style crease in my trousers, and had spit-shined my dress shoes to a mirror brightness—the Navy way. I had stood in his office doorway like I had so many times on Saturday mornings, like a boot awaiting inspection. He invited me to sit, and I listened intently to his description of my duties. I was to be paid the magnificent salary of $1.25 per hour for delivering orders all over town in the company's vans and green Ford station wagon, and for helping prepare orders for delivery in the warehouse. Although "Business" had never held any career interest for me, I applied myself to learning everything I could about the office supplies business, even in areas that didn't concern me. I learned about inventories, "FIFO and LIFO", bills of lading, wholesale vs. retail, drop shipments, and how to assemble chairs and other office equipment that came boxed as a dozen parts.

My first week, I rode shotgun with Jimmie "The Juice" Wyche, the Black senior delivery man who taught me the entire route downtown, including how to load the van with the last deliveries in the back and the earlier ones in front, as well as all the other tricks he knew. We laughed and joked a lot, and Jimmie took a liking to me, too.

I had called him "Mr. Wyche" at our first meeting, upon which he stopped and stared at me with a surprised expression. "Nobody never called me dat", he said after a moment. "Why you call me dat?"

"You're an older adult, and that's how I'm supposed to address you, sir", I responded. Jimmie was silent for a long time during our first trip.

"Where are you from, Mr. Steve?"

"Well, a bunch of places. My family traveled around a lot. I guess the closest thing to "home" is Missouri." I told him briefly about my childhood, my upbringing as a "Navy brat", and why I came to be working with him in a delivery van on that hot summer day. Jimmy was always extra nice to me after that day and did his best to ensure that I did everything correctly. He must have told the other drivers about our conversation, as well, because they all treated me as if I were special.

A month or so passed, and I must have been doing well because Mr. Sanford raised my pay to $1.50 per hour. One day, when I had a van to myself, I saw a new product arrive on the truck: a small, compact office swivel chair that retailed for the very low price of $29.00. I had helped assemble a few of them in the warehouse, and on impulse, I grabbed one and put it in the van. I had a sudden idea. There was a 10-story office building downtown, the bottom floor of which was occupied by the Barnett Bank. Other businesses occupied the remaining floors. Elevators had operators in those days, and the young women who operated them often had to be on their feet for long, painful hours every shift. I had noticed this, and that was the basis of my idea. The bottom line was that I returned to the store that day with four orders for those office chairs.

Mr. Sanford stammered when I asked him how to process the orders. "You did what?"

"Yes, sir, Mr. Sanford, I found four customers who want to order one of those new chairs that came in."

His mouth opened and closed, like a freshly caught trout, for a few moments. "Did they come to you to ask this?'

"No, sir. I just showed them one and explained how it was inexpensive but well-made for the price, and it sounded good, so they all wanted one. One office manager asked if he could get a discount if he bought five. I told him I'd ask you." An hour later, at closing time, Mr. Sanford had the sales staff gather in his office. I stood beside his desk, with one of the new chairs. After all five of our salesmen were present, Mr. Sanford cleared his throat and began. He told everyone what I had done and had me explain, in detail, how I had done it. During my speech, I had a sudden flashback to those many times I had stood and recited poetry to the Fall River Navy ladies. And that felt eerily similar to what was happening now. Mom had been showing me off. And Mr. Sanford was using me now to "motivate' his sales staff. Strangely, the salesmen, who were all family men and much older than I, did not receive my example well; they seemed, instead, to resent my accomplishment. Oh, well. Mr. Sanford not only paid me the standard 10% sales commission for my efforts, but he also raised my hourly rate to $1.75. I was on my way to paying for my first semester at JU! Plus, I learned that I had another ability of which I had been unaware: the power to persuade others.

My years at JU were formative. I kept my social life to a minimum, partly because of the bitter lessons I had learned about "distractions" at SEMO, but mostly because I had to keep working from here in the future, even as I studied, to pay for my education. Besides, Pi Kappa Alpha had no chapter at JU, so there were no frat brothers around to tempt me. I tried my hand at several jobs: manning the late shift at the In-and-Out, a tiny drive-in near campus that served hot dogs, French fries, fried shrimp, and other such food; I also mowed the neighbors' lawns for $2.00 per hour, and filled in at a car wash when I could. Every night, I came home smelling like grease and sweat, so I kept looking.

Finally, the job of my young lifetime was staring me in the face, in that morning's Help Wanted section. United Parcel Service (UPS), a Seattle-based delivery company that was slowly expanding across the country, was advertising for package handlers for all shifts at its new JAX Hub, which had just opened in the northern part of Jacksonville. The starting pay was $3.00 per hour, which was more than twice the minimum wage. I immediately borrowed a classmate's car and drove out to apply. ***And there's a small side story here, so let me pause in this particular narrative to tell it...***

***Have you ever been rewarded for an idea, y
ou stepped out upon to risk doing?
Why or why not?***

*For more on this topic, see Advanced Life Skills Syllabus Section V:
Rules of Success to Adopt Before Your 20's*

Did I Ever Tell You About...

HOW I DISCOVERED THAT HOMOSEXUALS REALLY EXISTED?

"Things are not always what they seem; the first appearance deceives many; the intelligence of a few perceives what has been carefully hidden."
—Roman fabulist Phaedrus

When I was still a junior at San Diego High School (1962), there was one kid in my class who seemed different from the others. I met him through the school Chess Team, of which I had been captain. Chess was one of those things that came naturally to me, and I was able to see two and three moves ahead, giving me a considerable advantage. We usually gathered to play during our lunch hour, on the tables laid out under the trees in a beautiful park on campus. Lennie was on the team and was a good chess player in his own right. I first noticed that something was strange when I observed, as he was moving a piece on the board, that Lennie's fingernails were carefully manicured and polished, like a girl's. His voice was rather high-pitched, and he kept his eyebrows neatly trimmed to a thin, dark line.

One day, as I was showing him the Budapest Gambit, his knee brushed against mine under the table. I thought nothing of it until I noticed that he did that a lot, and one day, he left it there, pressing against my leg. I looked up to find that he was staring at me, with a strange grin on his face. I moved to get up, and he said, "We don't have to quit yet, Steven. There's still ten minutes before next class".

I looked down at the board and replied, "No, I think we'd better stop now", and started to put our pieces back in the box.

He reached out and took hold of my hand. "Well, I just want you to know that I really like you, Steven, and I'd love it if we could spend some more time together. You know, after class."

And suddenly, I got it. My face felt hot, and I'm sure that I was blushing. I let out a ragged breath and said, "First off, Lennie, my name is not Steven, it's Steve. And I appreciate what you said, but I just don't have any spare time with homework, and all."

"Ok, I just want you to know that I'm always here if you change your mind." I walked back to my next class with a haste that surprised me. So there were "queers" around. Grandpa had told me that there were some men—and women—who didn't have normal attractions for the opposite sex, and that even the Bible spoke of them. They were called "queers" because they didn't have sex the way men and women normally do. My time on the farm had shown me, graphically, what "normal" sex was about, but I was still confused. Grandpa avoided any more details, and when I innocently asked him how men could possibly have sex with other men, he sighed and said, "Queers accept deliveries where normal men only make shipments." My young mind still couldn't wrap my head around such a notion, but he refused to provide any more details. Now, here came Lennie. And all those images that had clouded my young mind years before suddenly came into perspective. There really were such things as queers out there. But why would they approach me? This bothered me for some time.

Flash-forward to the matter of me borrowing a car to apply for a UPS job. I actually knew how to drive and had been driving the Sanford Delivery Van; I just had no license. For reasons I finally came to understand, Mom and Dad declined to teach me how to drive. I figured out that it was to protect me from "dating loose women", my mom's idea. However, my dad didn't want me driving the family VW because of the extra car insurance it would cost. We didn't have the money, he told me. So, when I finally started earning enough to pay my way, I hired a driving school to teach me the fine art of driving. I jumped when a horn honked in the driveway, and I ran out to meet my instructor. He had brought a behemoth of a car, a black 1960 Chrysler Imperial, with huge tailfins and a massive grille that resembled a giant, leering face. When I got in, I saw that there were two sets of brakes, one for the driver and one for the passenger.

"How do you do? I'm Dennis, your driving instructor. Are you Steven?" And when he pronounced my name that way, my flashback to Lennie was connected.

"I'm Steve, sir. Nice to meet you. Is this the car we'll be using?"

He nodded and continued, "Yes, Steve, it's got dual brakes so that I can stop the car in an emergency." I had gotten into the car on the passenger's side, but he got out and came around.

"You can go ahead and shift to the driver's seat, because you'll be doing the driving from here on today." We switched places, and Dennis instructed me slowly and carefully. The Chrysler Imperial was an absolute beast of an automobile. You had to drive it as if it were a boat; I could barely see over the hood, so Dennis fetched some cushions from the trunk for me to sit on. We sat in the driveway for some 10 minutes while Dennis explained and demonstrated the many controls the car featured. I had been used to riding in our tiny 1956 Volkswagen Beetle, "The Gronk", which was a model of simplicity. The speedometer dominated the tiny, flat dashboard; there was no gas gauge, and you only knew that the car was out of gas when the tiny engine started to cough and sputter, and then you had mere seconds to reach down and throw a lever that activated the reserve fuel supply, one gallon of gas. With the Beetle, Dad had told me, you could go 40 miles on that one gallon, and that was usually enough to get you to the next station. However, this Chrysler Behemoth had a gauge to measure how much fuel was left in its 20-gallon tank, as well as other indicators such as engine temperature, oil pressure, and various dials and switches that I did not understand but would soon learn to comprehend.

Dennis was a well-dressed man in his forties, friendly and talkative. He spoke with almost no break as we drove all over town, teaching me different maneuvers and situations. Parallel parking, which he labeled as the most difficult part for most people to learn, came naturally to me, and I passed that portion of my training with ease. As it turns out, my dad had taught me, very early on, how to handle a small boat: how to back into a tight space at the pier between other boats; how to back down slowly over a good fishing spot, and so on. Dad had been proud to see that I had a natural "seaman's eye", that is, a good instinct for judging time/speed/distance relationships, and adjusting my movements accordingly. I took to driving a car as quickly as I did to operating a small boat. Dennis noted this, and I only had to spend enough money for six hours of instruction over three days before he declared me ready to take the actual test, which I later passed with an almost-perfect score.

It was on my last day of instruction that Dennis revealed his "little secret", as he termed it. We were sitting under a tree in Boone Park, one of many small, isolated parks that the city maintained.

We were eating a fast-food lunch before taking my final training run, and Dennis started talking about his family life. "Our kids are all grown and gone, you know, but Glenda and I haven't slept together for years, not after she discovered my little secret". I was only pretending to listen; my attention was occupied by two squirrels that were squabbling over some tasty leftovers on the bench in front of the car. I was startled to look down and see Dennis's hand, attempting to unzip the front of my trousers.

I knocked his hand away and turned to face him: "What the hell are you doing, man?"

He had a sickening smile on his face. "That's my little secret, Steven. I really like nice young men like yourself. So, I want to give you a little graduation present. He reached for me again, and I jumped out of the car.

"How much do I owe you, sir?"

"Oh, call it part of my present. You're ready for the state test." Boone Park was only a few blocks from my house. Without another word, I started jogging back. Out of the corner of my eye, I saw that Dennis was driving slowly behind me. I stopped and turned around. "Please get away from me, or there's gonna be trouble, sir, and I'm not kidding!" I never saw nor heard from Dennis again. But that final piece of my education, the question I had asked long ago on the farm, was finally answered.

How has life surprised you as you grew up?
How did you face the dichotomy of what you
thought and what was real?

For more on this topic, see Advanced Life Skills Syllabus Section II:
Put on Your Full Armour for the Arena

Did I Ever Tell You About...

THAT I WAS (BRIEFLY) A RECORDING ARTIST?

*"Music is a hidden arithmetic exercise of the soul,
which does not know that it is counting."
— Gottfried Wilhelm Leibniz."*

I was immediately hired, several days after getting my driver's license, by UPS as a package handler. My formidable upper-body strength, built by long hours of farm work and physical training, gave me a distinct advantage. Because I worked the night shift, from 8:00 pm to 2:00 am, I was able to borrow my classmate Ollie's car until I could buy my own. He was more than happy with the arrangement, since he lived just a few blocks away, and I always topped off his tank before parking his car outside his folks' house and jogging home. The UPS job paid well enough that, before I knew it, I had saved enough to go car-shopping. The car that I picked was a mistake. To this day, I still can't understand what led me to choose the diminutive vehicle with the window sign that read, "RUNS GOOD, ONLY $325 AS-IS! DRIVE HOME TODAY!"

Looking back, it must have been the fact that I thought it looked "cute", sitting there alone, in the farthest corner of the used car lot, with tumbleweeds and trash accumulated around its tires. It reminded me of the runt beagle puppy in a litter, the one that nobody wanted, except me. I got in and started the engine, which sputtered a few times before coming to life, spewing a cloud of blue smoke from the tailpipe. "She ain't been started in a while, so that she might be a little stiff," said the lot man.

Stiff, indeed. I looked at the odometer, which read 66,000 and some miles. "Wow, that's not bad mileage!" I exclaimed, "How come it's got such low mileage? Has it been stored, or something?"

"Uh, no, son. It's been all the way around once already, so that's 166,000 miles on her. That's why she's only $325. But she runs good. Go on, take her for a spin." He had held my brand-new driver's license as security. Still, it also occurred to me that probably no one would bother stealing this little heap in the first place. My new runt beagle puppy was a 4-cylinder 1951 Anglia, an English Ford. It was flamingo-pink, had multiple patches of rust, and somehow reminded me of a giant pink rectal suppository. It had a three-speed manual transmission, with a gear shift that rose two feet off the floorboards. The heater did not work, which fact I overlooked, because it was still September, and quite warm. I took her across the Matthews Bridge and up onto I-95, the main artery through Jacksonville, which runs north and south. Once there, I pressed the pedal to the floor and waited… and waited. The speedometer needle finally rose, with painful slowness, to 55 mph hour—downhill—and refused to go any faster. Oh well, I thought, I'm sure I won't be getting any speeding tickets. I made my way back to the lot, pondering all the way back whether or not this was a good choice. The nostalgic comparison to an unwanted beagle puppy took over my logic. I chugged back into the lot, and before I knew it, I was counting out $20 bills on the counter of the office. The lot attendant gave me a temporary paper tag to tape in the rear window. I signed the necessary documents and was handed the title and keys. I drove home with my head up, my chest back, and my heart full of joy. My first car! "Beagle", as I named her, turned out to be an education all of itself.

I pulled Beagle into the driveway and walked proudly into the living room, where Mom and Dad were watching television. "Hey guess what, folks? I bought my first car!"

My parents sat for a moment, just staring at me. Dad slowly got up and walked out on the front porch to inspect my purchase. The remains of a cloud of blue smoke that Beagle had spewed as she came down our street were still hanging in the air. "Holy Mother of God, Steve! Do you mean to tell me that you actually paid good money for that pink piece of crap? How much?"

I recounted the deal to Pop, and he replied, "Well, I wish you'd have let me go over it first, but if it runs at all, that's probably a fair deal. However, you still need to get your own insurance.

"Yes, sir, I know. I already called Allstate, and they gave me a discount because our car insurance is already with them. It's only $26 per month to insure Beagle, and the agent said I didn't need a deductible, because it wasn't worth replacing or repairing if it was in a serious accident, so my insurance is only for injuries and such."

"That's called PIP, and I can see why", mumbled Pop. He asked me for the keys, and the irresistible curiosity of a natural mechanic led him to spend the next hour driving Beagle around the block, looking under the hood and the undercarriage, just checking everything out. He pronounced that the car was safe to drive, but that the rings were shot, and that it would burn oil like crazy, and that the shocks were worn out. "My advice is that you keep a case of 10/40 motor oil and a funnel in the trunk. You're gonna need it." Pop was right, of course, but I didn't care. For the first time in my young life, I had wheels!

Meanwhile, my first semester at JU was progressing well. My favorite class was History of Western Civilization, taught by a charming, mid-twentyish woman named Janice Jones. Miss Jones was a very cute, short brunette who was fond of wearing tight, fuzzy tops that highlighted her prominent bustline. She was delighted to learn that I knew both Latin and Greek, and allowed me to address the class a few times when we came to covering those parts of the curriculum. The student sitting to my left was a large, muscular young man in his early 30s by the name of Chuck Adams. We were introduced to each other on the first day, and Chuck had some interesting stories to share. He had spent four years in the US Marines and had seen actual hand-to-hand combat when the US intervened in Lebanon to quell a disturbance there. As I came to know him, I was fascinated by his stories of actual warfare and the hand-to-hand combat he had experienced. He, in turn, appreciated my recounting of the military upbringing I had at the hands of my dad. We became fast friends right away. So, when I noticed that Chuck couldn't keep his eyes off Miss Jones and wore a glassy-eyed grin as his head followed her around the classroom, I knew that my new friend was hopelessly hooked.

During our study sessions, he kept commenting about her in between topics like Charlemagne and the Battle of Hastings, and one day he just blurted out, "Steve, I'm gonna do it; I'm going to ask her out!"

"Who? Miss Jones?" I asked.

"Yes! She's absolutely the most beautiful woman I've ever seen." I looked up from my notepad.

"Chuck, buddy—I agree that she's all that. However, I believe there are non-fraternization rules in place. Even if she wanted to date you, she could get fired if you're caught, and you could get expelled." I could see from his dreamy-eyed expression that my words were falling on deaf ears.

"OK. Let's get back to work. The next question is:' Outline the major changes that William the Conqueror introduced to England after the Battle of Hastings, and analyze the effects of...." My voice trailed off as I saw that he was lost in his daydreams. I quietly mumbled goodnight and left Chuck sitting at the library table, staring into the distance.

The following Friday was the day of the Mid-Term Exam in Western European History. I was in my seat as soon as the doors were unlocked. Chuck walked in and took his seat next to mine. He was grinning from ear to ear,

"What?" I asked.

"I asked her out, and she accepted. But not until this semester is over."

"Great. Buddy! I'm happy for you!" was my heartfelt reply.

"I played my guitar for her over the phone, and she loved it. I'm in, Steve."

I stopped short. "You play guitar? I do too, a little. My dad taught me, and he's pretty good. We should jam some time. But let's get through this test first. Are you ready?"

Years earlier, Dad had taught me a few chords on the cheap guitar he bought for my 13th birthday. It came with a teach-yourself-guitar book, and I quickly took to the mathematical precision of the instrument. My dad liked country-western music, but I was drawn to the likes of Simon and Garfunkel, which was all the rage then. My young fingers quickly callused over from hours and hours of practice. I also discovered that I had a fairly decent alto/tenor singing voice, and soon Dad and I were thumping out songs together, a few of which he saved on a huge reel-to-reel tape recorder he kept in the sub-basement of our house, placed there at Mom's insistence. She preferred Montovani and Perry Como to any of our renditions, so we went down to the basement and closed the door to preserve the peace. The UPS job had blessed me with more money than I needed for school expenses, so I had treated myself to a used Martin twelve-string guitar. I was soon rendering the complex fingerings of "The Boxer" and similar songs with fairly decent competence. Dad even complimented me on my skill level, something he hardly ever did. There had always been a sort of distancing between Pop and me, something I didn't understand growing up, but was explained clearly when I turned 16. But that is another story…

To get to the point: Chuck Adams and Janice Jones started dating over the Christmas break, and the next thing I knew, they had eloped to Key West and returned as a married couple. Chuck had gotten a "B" in Western European History; he should have gotten an "A", but I later discovered that Janice had deliberately lowered his final score to avoid any accusations from the Faculty Advisory Board, which had somehow gotten wind of their dalliance and had them both under careful scrutiny. We started holding our practice sessions at the modest apartment home of Mr. and Mrs. Chuck Adams. Chuck and Janice were the two happiest people I had yet encountered, and when she started singing with us, her beautiful mezzo-soprano voice added a "Stevie Nix" flavor to our music. And shortly after that, my good buddy Ollie joined us with his banjo. I had not known about Ollie's ability with the banjo, and he hadn't thought to tell me. But play he could, and doggone well. The first night he joined our little group, we blended so well that it sounded downright professional. Janice, due to her teaching schedule, had classes on most of the same nights that we practiced. Since she was the sole breadwinner of the Jones family, we became the Montina Trio, complete with matching blue-checked Madras shirts and jeans to wear when we played in public; and play in public we did.

It was 1965, and as the Vietnam War escalated, the phenomenon of coffeehouses grew apace. It was the Age of the Flower Children. Bob Dylan, the Lovin' Spoonful, the Mamas and the Papas, the Beatles, and my beloved Simon & Garfunkel were all the rage, and their popularity grew in parallel with the growing opposition to the Vietnam War. We started playing at the dozen or so coffeehouses in and around downtown Jacksonville. To this day, I sometimes visit the Freedom Fountain on the banks of the mighty St. Johns River and reminisce. There used to be rows of coffeehouses where now stand multi-story parking garages and high-rise office buildings. Little do the present occupants know, but sixty years ago, that same area throbbed with the music of rebellion and anti-war songs, and the lively music of home-grown groups like the Montina Trio.

We were a hit, and soon we were raking in a hundred or so bucks a night in tips. The owners of these establishments loved to have us play, because their own businesses prospered when we did. One night, my mom and dad made a surprise visit to our 8:00 pm show, and I felt a swell of pride when they joined the standing ovation as we finished our show.

When I walked in the door later that night, Dad greeted me with, "You guys are really good, Steve. You need to cut a record. I know a studio where you can get it done for cheap." Again, a rare compliment from my dad. I could get used to this. But I knew he was sincere when he offered to pay the $250 fee for cutting our first record, on the condition that we pay it back as soon as we could. I agreed, and so began my illustrious—however brief—status as a Recording Artist. We all spent half a day at the studio, where, after multiple retakes, we finally cut a two-sided record with eight of our best songs on it. I kept staring at the label, savoring the satisfaction of seeing "The Montina Trio" proudly displayed on it. We knew nothing about marketing, however, and after nearly all of our friends and family bought a copy at $10.00 each, sales dried up. We sold several dozen at our performances, but that, too, slowly dwindled to a stop. In the end, we sold a total of 212 records. That's probably just as well, because any wider attention would probably have gotten us into trouble due to numerous copyright violations, of which we were blissfully unaware. But I've always been proud that, even for a brief moment in my time on this Earth, I was a folk-music star, and a bona-fide Recording Artist…

__Have you ever had someone believe in you enough to pay for a class or put up money for you to succeed? Who and when?__

For more on this topic, see: Advanced Life Skills Syllabus Section V: Rules or Success to Adopt Before Your 20s

Did I Ever Tell You About...

HOW I JOINED THE NAVY?

""War is a violent teacher."
— Thucydides,
History of the Peloponnesian War.

As I write this, I cannot help but notice the eerie similarity between my story and the classic movie *Forrest Gump*, starring the intrepid Tom Hanks. Like his character, I was swept up, along with many other young men, by the Vietnam Conflict. I felt a surge of patriotism at the thought of fighting for my country, but I also desperately wanted to earn my college degree. I sat and talked with my dad, man-to-man, who could not hide his interest in my military ambitions. We decided that I should join the Navy Reserves, which had a program that would allow me to sign an enlistment contract, enabling me to complete college and then serve two years on active duty.

Dad drove me down to the Navy Reserve Recruitment Center, and I was surprised to see a small tear in his eye after I took the oath and signed up on November 22nd, 1965. "I'm really proud of you, Steve." He said on the drive back. "More than you know. And I know that I've been hard on you. However, all that will now pay off. You're going into the Navy with a lot of know-how already under your belt. You'll do just fine. I know that you'll make your mom and me proud, and you already do."

And that was undoubtedly true. Pop and I went fishing on the weekends. In his small Boston Whaler, he taught me how to steer, the Coast Guard Rules of Inland Navigation, how to read tides and currents, and basic meteorology, as well as knot-tying, the elements of celestial navigation, and the numerous other details that a skilled seaman must master. And so it was that after a grueling two weeks of Boot Camp at Great Lakes Naval Station in February, I started what was to be my 30-year relationship with the United States Navy.

As my junior year progressed, I declared Ancient History as my major, and I was maintaining a solid 3.9 GPA without even trying hard. The Beagle had kicked the bucket, and the cost of repair exceeded the value of the car, which I had sold for scrap. Dad came to my rescue. His entire attitude towards me had changed dramatically after I had signed up. He openly bragged to his friends about my accomplishments. He came into my room and spoke for hours about things he had learned in the service, and I could see the excitement in his eyes when he talked of war and the lessons he had learned. He had also been offered a job as assistant manager of Budget Rent-A-Car, a new company just starting in Jacksonville. It represented a substantial career change for Pop, and he began earning more money than he had ever done before. One perk was a new car to drive as his own, and so it was that Gronk, our faithful 1956 Volkswagen Beetle, was offered to me for the princely sum of $500. Gronk was beautiful to my eyes. I had ridden in the back seat of this car for countless miles as we had crisscrossed the country. Gronk was battleship grey, had green leather upholstery, and was in immaculate condition. I know, because for years I had washed, waxed, vacuumed, and cleaned her from end to end. Now Gronk was mine! She had 168,000 miles on the odometer, but still ran like a Swiss watch. It felt as if she had always been mine.

However, as my first Reserve summer approached, I had two weeks in July circled; it was the time when my first summer of active duty would take place, on the *USS English* (DD-696), a Navy Reserve training ship anchored at Mayport Naval Station in Jacksonville. I reported aboard at 12:15 in the morning, having gone to a poolroom and bar called the Zanzibar for a rare drink or two with Ollie, Chuck, and Janice, who wanted to see me off. I had worn my brand-new Navy Tropical Dress White uniform, complete with E-2 (Seaman Apprentice) shoulder patch on my right arm, and a *"USS English"* patch on my left. My shoes were spit-shined to a mirror brightness, and my seabag was packed by Navy Regulations, which I knew almost by heart. As with my homeschooling long ago before Kindergarten, Pop had homeschooled me for this day. I already "spoke Navy", having grown up learning terms like head detail, reveille, port and starboard, two-blocked, scuttlebutt, chow line, and similar terminology already ingrained in my vocabulary. The Navy uses a LOT of acronyms; so many that they have published a dictionary, appropriately entitled DICNAVAB—the Dictionary of Naval Abbreviations. I had memorized it from end to end. On top of this, I had also passed the US Coast Guard Inland Navigation exam the year before my cruise. And my long years of Saturday morning inspections, plus growing up ALNAV, that is, "All Navy", had given me a huge advantage over the other recruits. Pop had taken me aboard every ship in which he served, from the time I was five, and I knew my way around a Navy vessel, from stem to stern. So, when I bid farewell to my friends on the pier, and walked up the gangway to the English's quarterdeck with my seabag on one shoulder, and saluted myself aboard, I was perfectly at home. The English was a veteran of WW II, a Sumner-class tin can (destroyer) with three twin-mounted 5" 38 guns and multiple smaller weapons.

I waited while the OOD signed me in. "You're not due to report until 0800 tomorrow, you know, Recruit. You're the first one to report. Everybody in your berthing compartment is already asleep, so I hope your night vision is good." He sent the BMOW (Boatsman's Mate of the Watch) with me to show me my bunk. It was after Lights Out, and everything below decks was lit only by red lamps. We carefully descended several ladders (stairs) and finally came to where a three-tiered set of bunks was bolted to the deck. My rack was the top one in one of these, but I could not stow my gear because the bottom bunk was firmly occupied by a snoring sailor whose bunk rested on top of my locker. So, I tossed my seabag onto the rack, pulled off my shoes, and crawled painfully into the tiny space between my rack and the overhead steel deck. I fell asleep, fully clothed, and drifted off to visions of me, standing proudly behind the wheel on the bridge, a dream that was soon to come true...

"NOW, REVEILLIE, REVEILLIE! ALL HANDS HEAVE OUT AND TRICE UP! THE SMOKING LAMP IS LIT IN ALL AUTHORIZED SPACES! NOW REVEILLE! MESS GEAR, CLEAR THE MESS DECK. SWEEPERS, SWEEPERS, MAN YOUR BROOMS! GIVE THE SHIP A CLEAN SWEEPDOWN FORE AND AFT! ALL RECRUITS WILL REPORT TO YOUR MUSTERING PETTY OFFICER ON THE FANTAIL AT 0800."

This thundering aural assault came from the 1MC (loudspeaker), which, unbeknownst to me, was mounted on a steel beam precisely three inches from my ear. I violently lifted my torso, only to bang my head painfully against the beam. Before I remembered where I was, I groaned, swung my legs over the edge of the bunk, and took a 6-foot step to the deck. My stocking-clad feet landed on a brass hatch cover that was bolted to the deck, and I suffered a nasty contusion when they landed squarely on the large brass bolts that ringed the hatch.

As I sat there, rubbing my feet and my head both, a messenger poked his head in the hatch, and said "Are you Mac Mickel?"

I nodded, and he said, "You've got quarterdeck watch as Messenger at 0745 am. Get yourself squared away and report on time."

"Aye-aye, sir." So, my first few hours on active duty did not go well. Things improved as the day progressed, and over the next few days, both my officers and petty officers were quite surprised that I had such a comprehensive understanding of the Navy from the start. It reminded me of my first day of Kindergarten, long ago and far away; and so it was. Our destination was Montego Bay, Jamaica. On the way, we conducted training exercises, chipped and applied paint, stood watch, and performed various training drills. I told my mustering Petty Officer, Boatswain's Mate First Class O'Connell, that I already knew the basics of Quartermaster, of which Pop had taught me.

"Well now, that's just wonderful, Recruit. But you're in First Division for now, and that means you're mine for now, and I want you to move your ass to the forecastle and grab a Red Devil, and start scraping that deck."

"Aye-aye, sir" I replied.

But O'Connel stopped me. "I'm not a 'sir', Recruit. I work for a living. You will address me as Petty Officer O'Connell, do you understand?"

"Yes, Petty Officer O'Connell." He smiled and watched me out of sight as I made my way forward to the forecastle. So, I spent the first full day on active duty on my hands and knees, scraping paint from the deck with a Red Devil scraper. By the time we broke for chow at 1100, my hands and knees were blistered, and my dungarees and blue chambray cotton shirt—the standard working uniform for enlisted men—were covered in paint chips and dust.

Chow was a new experience, as well. I quickly learned that the rank-conscious Navy fed you by your rank; petty officers ate first, and even they had a pecking order called "Right-arm Rates." Not only were we fed by the number of stripes we had, but I also learned that some rates, or categories of specialty, were considered superior to others, and so they got to stand in line ahead of those that were not. Among the Right-Arm Rates were Gunner's Mate, Boatswain's Mate, Radarman, Sonarman, and so on...the so-called "fighting" rates. Left-arm rates included Steward, Storekeeper, Personnelman, and others. This system had been officially abolished at the end of World War II. Still, the current skipper of the *English* was an old-fashioned traditionalist, and a US Navy Commanding Officer at sea is a fearsome thing—a man granted Divine-like powers—and so he did as he wished. Eventually, however, I got to stand underway deck watch on the bridge. My position was Lookout, and my duty station was on the port bridge wing. And this was my chance to show off.

I quickly demonstrated my command of Naval terminology and procedures; when I spotted an aircraft or surface vessel, I knew the proper way to report the same. "Unknown aircraft at 080, target angle 270 degrees, estimated altitude 1 mile, sir!"

The OOD replied, "Very well."

He walked over to the bridge wing, raised his binoculars, and confirmed my report. He turned to glance at my name badge. "That's very good, Recruit McMickley. Where did you learn correct procedure for that report?"

"Thank you, sir. It's pronounced McMikle, sir, and I learned from my father, who was a Chief Quartermaster, sir!"

"Navy brat, eh? Well, that's very good. ALNAV, eh?"

"Yes SIR!" I replied. From that day on, word spread about the new Recruit who was already an accomplished watch-stander. The next day, I found myself standing in front of the XO's desk, at attention.

"At ease, McMikle. I'm see here that you're quite knowledgeable regarding bridge watch procedures, and that your father was a career Quartermaster. Is this true?"

"Yes sir. My dad trained me growing up. I already passed the Coast Guard Inshore Navigation exam, and I request permission to strike for Quartermaster, myself, sir."

The XO sat and sized me up for a moment. "Well, it does seem a shame to waste such talent on scraping paint. OK, Mr. Allen. Please start the process for allowing this man to strike for QM, and I'll forward it up the chain. Atten-CHUN!"

We snapped to attention before he dismissed us. LT Allen was the SWO—Senior Watch Officer. He was also the head of the WEPS (Weapons) Department. He pulled me aside as we stood in the passageway outside the XO's stateroom. "I hope you realized that I stuck my neck out for you, McMikle. Do you have any idea how rare it is to be allowed to strike as an E-2? If you let me down, I can guarantee that you'll scrape paint for the rest of this cruise."

I smiled and nodded. "I won't let you down, sir. You have my word on it."

And I certainly didn't. By the time we reached Montego Bay, I had qualified as Lookout, Helmsman, Lee Helm (the "throttle") Operator. I was even able to solve Maneuvering Board problems—something unheard of in new Recruits on their first underway deployments. The maneuvering board was a 16" x 16" sheet of paper pre-printed with a compass rose and grid lines, used in conjunction with a set of navigation instruments to manually calculate the course and speed changes necessary to perform station changes in a formation of ships underway. As several senior Petty Officers watched, I demonstrated my ability to solve complex, multi-ship station changes with practiced ease; Pop had taught me years earlier, and now that training paid off.

"He's a natural, Skipper," I hadn't noticed that the XO and CO and had joined us on the bridge,

"That's great, gentlemen. XO, transfer this man to OPS immediately. Good work, McMikle."

"Thank you very much, sir" I glanced at LT Allen, who winked at me as I saluted smartly before leaving the bridge.

Jamaica was the first of many foreign countries that I was to visit over the next 30 years. I, of course, enjoyed the experience, but the highlight of my first cruise was my deep sense of pride as I sewed my QM striker designation patch onto my uniform. And when, days later, I walked into my parents' living room and showed my dad my QM insignia, he smiled broadly and gave me a long hug—something else that had been very rare growing up. That was the happiest moment of my life, thus far. And so began my 30-year stint in the United States Navy.

What assets have you been given from people with more experience than yourself? How have you used those skills?

For more on this topic, see Advanced Life Skills Syllabus Section IV: Universal Laws, Hiding in Plain Sight

Did I Ever Tell You About...

THE SHOCK OF MY LIFE?

"Know thyself."
— *Inscription at the Temple of Apollo at Delphi,
traditionally attributed to the Seven Sages of Greece.*

I soon developed and established what was to become my regular routine over the next four years. And in doing so, I also learned an important lesson that would become an integral part of my life in every respect. I had long ago figured out that I displayed all the symptoms of OCD—Obsessive-Compulsive Disorder. From my obsession with not stepping on sidewalk cracks to my habit of automatically waking up at a predetermined time, without an alarm clock, my daily routines, functions, and actions were something that I could perform even while in a brain fog. I fit every definition of a "nerd"; I was predictable, habitual, and boringly self-programmed.

My reputation as the "Boy Scout" had stuck with me and would remain so, up until the present day. But I have also managed to become very productive as a result. And this is worth all of the abuse and accusations I have withstood. With this respect of being so "straight" has come a philosophy which I have entitled FOPO/IDM: Fear of Other People's Opinions was not something to which I chose to subject myself, because IT DIDN'T MATTER. Looking back, I have lived a life embodied by Frank Sinatra's iconic song, "I Did It My Way", and Ricky Nelson's "Garden Party", the tagline for which is, "…you can't please everyone, so you've got to please yourself." So true, so very, very true. And yet, every generation seems to fall all over itself re-learning—or NOT LEARNING—this basic hypothesis. One need only look at the legions of people, both young and old, who live or die every day based on the number of "likes" they receive on Facebook. The downfall of many is that they genuinely believe they require approval from total strangers before moving ahead with a plan or idea. Oh, well.

As I progressed toward my goal, I began to consider making the Navy a career. And, halfway through my junior year, this possibility became even more likely when I came home from my shift at UPS at 11:30 at night, only to find my mom and dad still awake and waiting for me at the kitchen table. "We waited up because something really important came in the mail today." I poured myself a cup of coffee—which had become my drug of choice since starting college—and sat down as Dad pushed a letter over to me. It had my riveted attention as soon as I saw the letterhead, the starred blue pennant at the top, and the imprimatur of a Navy Rear Admiral: it was a letter addressed to Dad from Rear Admiral Draper Kaufmann. My dad had apparently written to the Admiral, and this was his response:

"Dear Chief McMikle: I am delighted to inform you that, in response to your inquiry to me of 19 NOV 1966, I have managed to secure an appointment for your son, Steven, to the summer class of the United States Officer Candidate School in Newport, Rhode Island. He will soon be receiving orders to report for the first six-week class, beginning on May 16, 1966. Congratulations, Chief McMikle. If he turns into half the sailor you are, the Navy will be lucky to have him. My very best wishes for his success. Respectfully, etc, etc."

I was stunned. I never saw this coming, and suddenly I knew that the Navy and I were about to be bonded forever. Officer Candidate School! I had joined primarily to avoid being drafted into the Army and becoming another piece of raw meat for the Vietnam grinder, without even finishing college. I had, just a month before, sewn on my "crow", the proud eagle and chevron insignia of a United States Navy Petty Officer Third Class Quartermaster. To no one's surprise, I had passed the QM3 exam with a near-perfect score. This is probably the variable that pushed me over the top.

Still, Rear Admiral Kaufman had been one of Pop's commanding officers on one of the many ships in which he had served. I remember reading the glowing performance report that Dad had received from the Admiral upon his transfer. This probably helped, as well.

Pop couldn't stifle his smile of pride when he warned me, "Now, don't expect me to salute you, Boot. But congratulations, not none. He stood up and extended his right hand. "Your mom and I are proud of you, Steve. I know you won't let us down." He couldn't hide the tiny tears that formed in his eyes. Dad had never expressed much emotion toward me, something that I never fully understood until my 16th birthday: September 15, 1961. Pop had been stationed on a heavy cruiser, homeported in San Diego, California, and I had just started my junior year at San Diego High School. I had received several items of new clothing from my parents, and these were welcome, indeed. Up until that year, most of my clothes were bought at thrift stores or sewn by hand from curtain material. But after we cut the cake and I blew out my candles, a somber mood settled on both their faces, and I discerned that something negative was coming.

Dad cleared his throat and began. "There's something that you need to know, Steve. Something that we probably should have told you a long time ago, but we wanted to wait until you were old enough to handle it." Now, a feeling of real foreboding began, and I felt my heart pounding in my eardrums. They were clearly uncomfortable, and my mom looked down at her lap, shaking her head. Then dad just blurted out, "I'M NOT YOUR REAL FATHER, STEVE. There's a long story we have to tell you. And I want you to know that we both love you very much, but we couldn't wait any longer to tell you." For the next hour, although I had to get up early for class the next day, I sat in silence as the story unfolded.

Mom and Dad had met in elementary school, in a one-room schoolhouse in Illmo, a town with a population of 870. I was born in a Quonset Hut, a zinc-coated steel half-cylinder that was the military's quick and easy solution for instant buildings, where they were needed. This make-shift hospital was located on a US Army Air Corps base in Tucson, Arizona. I had often wondered why Mom and Dad had been on an Army base, and this one was the site of an Army Air Corps Gunnery School for bomber crews. But I had just let it go. As the story unfolded, Mom had been there with her first husband—and my biological father—whose name, I learned, was Marshall Emil Hirsch.

Mom stopped and pulled out my birth certificate from a tattered photo album, which I had never seen until that moment. It stated that my name at birth was Steven Warren Hirsch. A chill ran up my spine. As it turns out, Marshal Hirsch and my "dad" had been rival suitors for Mom in that one-room schoolhouse. "Pop" had been one of six unwanted children born to one Eilleen MacGlachlan, who was what folks back then called a "loose woman." His paternal father had been a man by the name of David McMikle, one of Eileen's many dalliances. He had named me Steven before he moved to Idaho, after Eilleen had moved on to another "boyfriend." My Pop's life growing up, as Grandpa eventually told me, was one of hard-scrabble poverty and unending work, with a mother who was that in name only. Pop grew up unloved and unwanted. He had met Mom in that one-room schoolhouse at the same time that Marshall did. They both ardently courted my mother, and they both had joined the military right out of school; Marshall wanted to fly, so he joined the Army Air Corps. Dad went into the Navy after graduating from the 11th grade, so he never received his diploma. As he later recounted, the Navy became his mother, providing him with the only home he had ever known, up to that point. Marshall became a B-17 bomber radio operator and waist gunner (which is why he had been stationed at the Tucson Gunnery School when I was born). He had married Mom a year before, who had finally chosen "the other guy" to marry, and as soon as I was born, Marshall had abandoned my mom, and neither wrote nor called her from that moment on. Mom had been heartbroken, but Bill McMikle still loved my mom very much, and they were married when Dad came home to Illmo on a two-week leave and had a tearful reunion. Mom had had her first marriage annulled, and the proof of Bill's devotion to her came when he had willingly adopted the son of his bitter rival as his own. When it had become clear that Marshall had abandoned my mom, she took me back to Illmo and the farm. As I sat and listened in silence, so many things had become clear, and when the moment came when they pulled out Marshall's pictures, I was horrified to see that—OMG!—I was the spitting image of him! No wonder that Pop had been so "distant" from me all my life! Many years later, after Pop had died in 1995, I finally tracked down my "other" family in Long Island, New York. But that is another story. So, this was the reason that Pop had never called me "son"—I wasn't!

But, back to the Navy—

I eagerly reported to Newport, Rhode Island, for Naval OCS training the following May, my head full of dreams and my eyes seeing stars on my shoulder boards. As with boot camp, I took to Navy OCS like a duck to water. In my Hotel Company class of 455 Officer Candidates, I ranked #3 from the top after my first six weeks, in every area but one: Engineering. I have since come to understand how God confers blessings. Our Creator has endowed each person in His creation with unique talents. Almost everyone is good at something; in my case, my special blessing was a condition that I have since learned is known as *synaesthesia*. Apparently, it's quite rare, only appearing in some form in less than .25% of the general population.

My version of synaesthesia is the ability to remember and retain words, definitions, fine details, and rules of grammar in multiple foreign languages. It is closely connected to the same cognitive ability that confers a natural talent for music, which I already knew that I had. Wolfgang Amadeus Mozart is said to have had this gift, as well, and he wrote his first full-scale piano composition at the age of 8. The downside of this arrangement is that I had been given almost "zero" ability in mechanics and high-order technology, try as I might to learn. Dad had always chided me for not delighting in changing oil, or cleaning spark plugs, or all the other DIY skills of the backyard mechanic. It had zero appeal, to match my zero skills. So, in my OCS Engineering courses, I barely managed to achieve a 78.5% score. It was that one disparity that kept me from getting a perfect 4.0 across the board. I arrived back home and took the idle few weeks before the Fall semester of my last year at JU to begin relaxing and taking stock of where I was, career-wise.

I had long since discovered that archaeology, my former dream profession, was a loser in terms of financial rewards. There was no money to be made, unless you taught it at some university; even if one managed to snare one of the rare grants or exploratory expeditions available, these were short-lived and were doled out to a small circle of pipe-smoking insiders. I had ambitious plans, and my entrepreneurial sense had endowed me with a hunger to make enough money to fund those plans. So, I signed up for some business classes.

My counselor commented on the unusual combination of classes I had enrolled in for the next semester: Botany II/Mycology, Advanced German, Basic Accounting and Bookkeeping, Golf, Cultural Anthropology, and Business Law. "That's a rather unusual blend, Steven. What do you plan to pursue with all this?" he asked.

"Well, sir, I'm still trying to decide, but I'm preparing to be able to afford to do what I enjoy, by getting good at some things that I don't enjoy, but need to know so that I can earn enough to make that happen."

"Interesting", replied Mr. Gooding, as he peered at me over my application form from across his desk. "Well, you'll certainly be well-rounded…but don't you think it's important to specialize and be more focused?"

"That would be true if life made that easy to do. But life really doesn't often offer us that option, does it, sir? I want to be ready for whatever comes my way, that looks worth pursuing".

So it was that, in April of 1968, when I had completed my second six weeks of OCS and graduated to become an Ensign in the United States Navy right after I had received my BA in Ancient History, that my "Dream Sheet" confirmed my worst nightmare. I was in the top tier of my OCS graduating class, and the Vietnam Conflict was in full swing. We were allowed to choose a theater (location), a ship type, and a department. My choices were perfectly natural, at least to me. I listed West Coast (which translated to Vietnam) as my choice of theater; small combatant (destroyers) as my ship type; and Operations (OPS) as my choice of Department. In a destroyer, the Departments consist of OPS, WEPS (Weapons), SUP (Supply, which was in charge of pay and logistics), and ENG, which kept the mechanical side of things running. Although everything on my qualification sheet positively screamed out "Operations", my Detailer (the faceless bureaucrat who sits behind a desk in the bowels of the Pentagon and decides such things) assigned my life for the next two years to be: West Coast/Vietnam (great!); the *USS Scofield* (DEG-3), a brand-new guided missile frigate as my ship type (also great!); and Damage Control Assistant (DCA) in the Engineering Department as my position (awful!). AAAAARGH! My worst nightmare of an assignment had come to pass!

Yes, I could go fight in Vietnam; and yes, I was assigned to a vessel designed to go in harm's way; but "DCA" evoked all those bad memories of standing stooped-over, with sweat dripping into my eyes, with an oily rag and wrench at Gronk's engine, while dad chewed on me for not loving all things hot, greasy, oil-covered, and knuckle-busting…but as they said in the days of sail: *"Growl ye may, but go ye must"*.

What experience have you had in your life when what you thought you knew you didn't know?

For more on this topic, see Advanced Life Skills Syllabus Section II: Put on Your Full Armour for the Arena

Did I Ever Tell You About...

THE TIME I WAS SUNK IN PEARL HARBOR?

*"An entire sea of water can't sink a ship unless it gets inside the ship.
Similarly, the negativity of the world can't put you down
unless you allow it to get inside you."*
— *Goi Nasu*

Whenever I drop that little gem in public, someone usually interrupts with some version of: "...now wait just one minute! You're not old enough to be a Pearl Harbor survivor! So how could you possibly have been there? What ship were you on?"

To which I respond, "On the Captain's gig of the *USS Schofield*." And yes, it's true. The blank stares that inevitably follow demand an explanation; so here it is...

I had reported aboard the *USS Schofield* (DEG-3) in November of 1968, having gone from OCS directly into the Navy's 8-week DCA Officer School at Philadelphia Navy Yard, followed by another 4 weeks at Pressure-Fired Boiler School, housed in the same vast, red-brick building. Both of these courses were designed to transform me into a bona fide Naval Engineer. I was given two weeks to report to my ship after completing all this training, to say my farewells and attend to personal business. I will never forget the day I walked in the front door of our home in my brand-new Service dress Kakhi uniform, complete with my first and only medal—the American Defense Medal. This small red-and-yellow piece of cloth—which everyone who takes the oath gets, just so they have at least one—was referred to as a "gedunk" medal, i.e., meaningless. But I wore it with pride nonetheless. Mom and Dad stood up, and we had a long group hug. Dad couldn't conceal his pride in my accomplishment, and Mom couldn't stop crying. It was the happiest moment of my life, up to that point. I had saved my Ensign's salary, and armed with a $2,000 cash budget, Dad took me down to the VW dealership where he had worked as Assistant Service Manager: I drove away in my brand-new 1969 white Volkswagen Beetle. Dad had persuaded the salesman to cut me his best deal, so for the princely sum of $2,002, I proudly drove Marshmallow (the name I gave her) back to the house. Gronk had died when I had foolishly driven her onto the beach with my girlfriend and gotten sand into the transmission. The girl I had been dating, Francesca, gave me a farewell kiss when, a few days later, I began my road trip to Long Beach, California, where *Schofield* was docked. We were scheduled to deploy to South Vietnamese waters after a weapons load-out at Pearl Harbor, which explains my presence in Pearl Harbor, where I was, indeed, sunk.

I had adapted to the wide range of personalities in the Wardroom rather quickly. The skipper, a crusty Commander with a reputation as a "screamer" (someone who yells a lot), was distant with everybody; my Senior Watch Officer was a kindly, easy-going senior Lieutenant who became sort of a father-figure for me; I also met the other department heads and officers. We had a wide variety of personalities. And then there was the XO, a bald Lieutenant Commander who was ready to retire. I shall, out of respect for their privacy, leave them anonymous, since many of them are still living. Suffice it to say that we all got along reasonably well, but that I was immediately assigned to the lowly status of "George". This was a Naval tradition that Pop hadn't told me about, but that I was about to painfully learn.

Every ship in the Navy has a pecking order, and you carry your position within that pecking order for every function on the ship. "George" is the lowest-ranking Ensign in the Wardroom. George is assigned to all those "collateral" duties, i.e., jobs that are general in nature and almost always undesirable. As George, my collateral duties included being Mess Caterer, Entertainment Coordinator, and general messenger for every picayune task that came along.

As DCA, I also served as Electrical Officer, Movie Officer, Salvage Officer, and Auxiliaries Officer. What this meant was that, if anything broke, my job was to have it fixed. To be George is to be a creature at once pitied and abused. The heartfelt dream of every George is to see the arrival on board of an Ensign to whom he holds seniority, and so hands off the miserable functions of that office to the "Newbie". But I was still George on the night before we were due to deploy to Midway Island to refuel, and from there to our destiny, fighting the bloody war in Vietnam.

I was sound asleep in my stateroom after an exhausting 16-hour day, spent making final preparations to get underway in the morning. "Steve, Steve!" and a gentle shaking of my arm by the XO, who strikingly resembled "Mr. Clean", without the earring. I shook myself awake and blinked before responding,

"Yessir?"

"Aren't you the Salvage Officer? You know, as one of your collateral duties?" Now I was wide awake.

"Yes, sir, I believe that I am."

"Outstanding! Report to the OOD on the quarterdeck, on the double."

"Aye-aye, XO." In a matter of moments, I was dressed and standing before LTJG Louis. "Reporting as ordered, Sir." Jimmy Louis had become my friend, but those things are forgotten when emergencies come to pass. He explained, in hushed tones, what had happened in the past few hours. The CO had taken his gig (his personal boat) over to the Oahu shore to visit a friend before deploying, and the coxswain (the man who operates the boat), who had left the Captain ashore, was called back to the ship. This sailor had performed what is called "cutting a buoy" on his return to the ship. Cutting a buoy meant that he had taken a shortcut and ignored the hazard to navigation that the buoy marked. It also meant that he had taken a risk in the interest of haste.

The result was that the Captain's gig had hit a hidden coral snag and torn the bottom out of the hull. The gig was literally sunk in five feet of water, surrounded by much deeper water on all sides. Since the Navy could not permit one of its vessels, however small, to remain unmanned at sea, my job was to "man the ship" until the salvage barge came in the morning to retrieve it. I was deposited on the half-sunken gig at 0330 in the morning; the barge was due to arrive at 0700. So, my task was to stand watch on the gig until then. The job seemed simple enough, but I was cold, tired, and hungry from the previous day's labors, and found myself rummaging through the emergency rations for a snack. The dates on some of those packets were from WW II, so I decided that it wasn't worth the risk of ptomaine poisoning. There were also 40-year-old packs of Lucky Strike cigarettes. I didn't smoke often, but needed some way to stay awake, so I ripped open a pack of Luckies and lit up...only to begin a coughing spasm that lasted several minutes. I did manage to remain awake on my tiny "first command." Even so, just before dawn, I couldn't keep my eyes open, and the accumulated fatigue of the last 48 hours finally claimed me. I drifted off, in a sitting position, on the horseshoe-shaped couch—which was just above the water level…

…only to be violently thrown to one side when the boat was suddenly lifted out of the water by the stern ring, which was attached to the crane on the salvage barge, which had silently motored up to me.

I stuck halfway out of the port window, and I yelled at the helmeted dock worker who was steadying the winch line. "HEY! HEY! There's somebody on the boat! Lower it back!", the worker yelled at the crane operator, who dutifully lowered the gig back into the water…right into the deep part, that was on all sides of the coral snag. Down I went, still clinging to the open window. I figured that I was roughly 20 feet down when I managed to swim out of that window and splutter to the surface. They threw me a line, by which I clambered back onto the barge, my uniform smeared with oil and grease stains. ***Nevertheless, I am able to honestly claim that I was sunk in Pearl Harbor… and lived to tell the tale.***

***Where have you been and nobody knew,
or those who knew would share a clue?***

*For more on this topic, see Advanced Life Skills Syllabus Section I:
Effective Human Communications*

Did I Ever Tell You About...

WHAT IT'S LIKE TO BE IN A REAL SHOOTING WAR?

*"Amid the arrows falling like rain,
let your mind stand firm, for panic kills sooner than steel."
— Modern paraphrase in the spirit
of ancient Stoic and military wisdom.*

You read about war all your life. You watch movies like *Sergeant York*, starring Gary Cooper, and *Beau Geste*, as well as *Midway*, starring Charlton Heston, and form ideas and opinions about war. Being a Navy Brat, I was more familiar with descriptions of actual warfare than most young men. I never knew it growing up, but my father, William Edward McMikle (whom everyone, including my mom, had nicknamed "Dub" for W.E.), was a genuine war hero. It was years later, after I had returned from my first Gulf War tour, that I went home on leave with a copy of *Saving Private Ryan*, starring Tom Hanks, for my parents to watch. Mom and I had both known that "Dub" had taken part in the Big War, in both Europe and the Pacific. But neither of us had known the full story of the part that he had played, because he had never spoken of it. So, when I inserted the tape of Private Ryan into the video player, both my mother and I were totally unprepared for what happened next.

We were several minutes into the first part of the film, wherein the hapless soldiers coming ashore were being massacred by German machine guns and artillery at Omaha Beach, on D-Day, June 6th, 1944. Pop suddenly jumped up and ran, sobbing, from the room. He went into the bathroom and closed the door, but we could hear him, still crying and shaking uncontrollably.

"Dub? Honey? What's the matter?" Mom drummed on the door.

"Turn it off! Turn it off! I can't watch it. Please turn it off!" I hastened to obey. Pop eventually came out, first checking to ensure that we had done as he asked. As he sat, with mom rubbing his trembling shoulders, he told us his long-suppressed story.

Dad had joined the Navy to escape his miserable life as another throwaway offspring of Ms. MacGlachlan. He grew up hard and tough, and the Navy provided the only real family he had ever known. Mrs. MacGlachlan gladly signed the underage waiver required for someone only 17 years old to join up; she had been happy to get rid of him, and Pop was equally happy to leave. He finished boot camp and became a Signalman striker, a sailor who was to master Morse code and flashing light, semaphore, using red-and-yellow signal flags to send silent messages, and signal flag communications hoisted on heavy lanyards, hung on the mast. These skills are still in use today because when the power goes out, all those miracle tech gadgets are useless. Signalmen provide the only way to communicate between and among ships at sea when all else fails. Pop had been a natural for this job. He had Popeye forearms, so the grueling task of hoisting and re-hoisting hundred-pound strings of wet signal flags was easy for him. His scores on the flashing light test had been exemplary, so he had rapidly mastered this vital skill set. And so, Dad was assigned to LST 235 as Seaman Signalman. The ship was stuffed with trucks and jeeps and had followed the second wave onto Omaha Beach, and into the Hell on Earth that was to follow.

"It was the most terrible thing I've ever seen. The screams, the guts scattered all over, the gunfire, the men begging to be shot because of their pain." He told us in a shaking voice, after he had managed to calm down, how, after discharging their loads, the 140 LSTs at Omaha Beach were assigned to MEDEVAC duty, tasked to remove the mangled bodies of terribly wounded men, both ours and the enemy's, to safety back across the English Channel. He also later told us that the movie was so incredibly accurate, and how the whistling bullets and screams of the dying took him on a terrible flashback to that awful event, so long ago and far away. There was no such thing as "PTSD"—Post Traumatic Stress Disorder—back then. It was termed "shell shock", and was considered to be an untreatable condition that was more of an "inconvenience' than anything else. However, Pop had definitely acquired it at Omaha Beach. My opinion of him rose to heights I had not predicted when he had started my Saturday inspections, so long ago.

The *Schofield* pulled into Midway Island to refuel and regroup, then reported to Yankee Station, an invisible point in the middle of the Gulf of Tonkin, where our primary task was to escort attack aircraft carriers that were launching and recovering 24-hour airstrikes inshore on the mainland. We were assigned to DESRON 23, the "Little Beavers", a WW II vintage destroyer squadron with a proud action history. In fact, several of our squadron-mates were veterans of WW II, destroyers that had seen action at Guadalcanal, and the Battle of the Coral Sea, and many other encounters which had left them with an impressive row of battle stars, proudly displayed below the bridge. Our primary task was Anti-Submarine (ASW) and Anti-Aircraft warfare (AAW) defense cover for the carriers, as they rained death and destruction on the enemy. *Schofield* was the only Little Beaver that was literally designed, from the keel up, to fulfil both tasks. She was fitted with the new Tartar anti-aircraft missile system, capable of shooting down air targets at a range of ten miles, and also engaging surface targets, utilizing the new SPA-52 height-finding radar system. For submarine threats, we also had the new SQS-26 sonar system, an ASROC missile system that was nuclear-capable, a drone helicopter capable of hovering over submerged targets and delivering torpedoes on target, and even a stern-firing, state-of-the-art acoustic torpedo. *Schofield* was #3 in what was called the *Brooke-clas*s of 6 destroyer-missile-firing Escorts. This was an experimental platform for several spanking-new weapon systems that the Navy had developed. Our main gun, however, was a vintage 5"/38 caliber naval cannon from WWII. Our sister ships, the *Brooke, Ramsey,* and three more like us, were launched to see what worked and what did not.

Day after day, for weeks at a time, we launched and recovered, launched and recovered, on a 24-hour basis. Everyone on board, from the CO down, was exhausted when we finally received orders to report to Subic Bay, Philippines, for R&R and replenishment. Subic Bay and its port town of Olangapo City consisted of a long, dirt-paved street lined with rows of sailor bars, cheap hotels, and cheaper restaurants, which were there to cater to the thousands of sailors and airmen who were fighting the Vietnam War. And cater they did. I will provide no details other than to say that, during an alcoholic haze that I had not experienced since my days at SEMO, I hooked up with a pretty young Filipina named Marietta. She was a sweet, innocent-looking (LOL), 19-year-old "island girl". She fulfilled fantasies that I did not know existed. I became her "Butterfly Boy" for the rest of that deployment. And Marietta succeeded, over several R&Rs in the next few months, in completing my Sex Education…in which she must have held, at the very least, a PhD. Some nights, I still see her smiling face, and smile back in my dreams…BOOOOM!

...I was shaken back to the grim reality of warfare by a huge fireball which erupted in my binoculars. I was standing the midwatch (1145-0345) on the bridge, as Junior Officer of the Deck (JOOD). We had been steaming 1,000 yards (about ½ mile) behind the carrier, recovering a flight of A-6 Intruder bombers returning from dropping their gifts on the enemy. The words "Roger Ball, Home Court" came from the last Intruder pilot, who was approaching to land on the deck of the *USS Bonhomme Richard* (CVA-31), AKA the "Bonny Dick". These words meant that the pilot had seen the "meatball"—a red light that indicated that he was properly aligned to land. The explosion occurred as his plane struck the fantail of the carrier.

The OOD and I leaped across the bridge to the 1MC and yelled, "NOW HEAR THIS! NOW HEAR THIS! PILOT IN THE WATER! AWAY THE EMERGENCY RESCUE DETAIL THIS IS NOT A DRILL, I SAY AGAIN, THIS IS NOT A DRILL!" This was the price paid when exhausted men, carrying out a demanding schedule, that never seemed to end, miscalculated due to fatigue. The *Schofield* swung into action to perform the task which was our primary mission: plane-guarding—in this instance, rescuing downed pilots from the ocean. We launched into the standard routine emergency search pattern, while the "Bonny Dick" abruptly changed course to clear the area, and our search for the lost pilot began. We had been circling, searchlights frantically scanning the wavetops and extra lookouts deployed, for about twenty minutes, when we received this terse message from the carrier: "PILOT ON BOARD".

What had happened, in that heart-stopping instant before the fireball, was that the pilot had realized he was going to crash, and ejected! Carriers display minimum lighting on the flight deck during nighttime launch/recovery operations, so as not to provide any enemy submarines with a well-lit silhouette, at which to launch a torpedo attack. That was the other part of *Schofield's* job on this mission: to provide ASW (anti-submarine) protection. And when that pilot had ejected, he had come down in the shadow of the "island"—the relatively small superstructure containing the bridge and air operations equipment which rose above the flight deck. He had been knocked unconscious when he landed and was literally sleeping, undetected, in the darkness at the base of the island. As the Officer of the Deck shouted orders to stand down from rescue OPS, I was still so adrenaline-pumped that I could barely stop shaking enough to record the incident in the log. But as I reflect now on that incident, so long ago and far away, it serves as a reminder of how easy it is to forget that, after all the recruiting fanfare, flag-waving, training and drilling, and rushing to-and-fro, the military profession is all about one thing, and one thing only: the give and take of DEATH.

We spent a total of 6 1/2 months in that WESPAC deployment, the highlights of which included a two-week stint as Station Ship Hong Kong and a real adventure that involved an unplanned, unwanted "vacation." We were anchored at Kaoshiung, Taiwan. We were due to report back to Yankee Station in two days, and the Engineering Officer, my department head, sent me ashore to have the package conveyor motor rewound. This was to be paid with a voucher at a local electrical repair shop. He was very specific that I was not to return without the repaired motor. I sat in a nearby bar until a boy ran in to say that the motor was finished. As I walked back to the shop, one of those strange feelings of foreboding came over me. And sure enough, as I returned to the rickety pier where the ship's motor whaleboat and coxswain had been waiting, my dread was confirmed. The pier was empty!

The *Schofield* appeared as a rapidly shrinking silhouette on the horizon, and a young boy handed me a hastily scribbled note on the back of an envelope. "Emergency orders. Underway ASAP. Meet us in Yokosuka (Japan) on AUGUST 29TH." OMG! I was guilty of "Missing Movement", which is a nearly unforgivable offence for an officer, especially in wartime, to commit. Nice career move, Stevie!, I thought. Oh well. I quickly took inventory of my situation. I was wearing my Working Kakhi uniform, had my US Navy ID card, a $20 bill folded up inside my shoe, my blue ball cap, and a pair of Naval Aviator sunglasses. Not much in terms of supplies and equipment, and… oh, yes! I also had that 40-pound motor, which I carried by a single canvas strap. This was, to date, the lowest point in my Navy career. It would also be the beginning of a two-week odyssey across the Far East.

So, I put on my Boy Scout hat and considered my position. I spoke no Mandarin Chinese, but most of them spoke English. My first objectives were food and shelter. Twenty dollars, even in 1969 Taiwan, wouldn't go far. I looked out into the harbor and spotted the *USS Nicholas* (DD-449), an old WW II Fletcher-class destroyer, swinging at anchor.

Aha! A Navy resource! I was saved. Or so I thought…

**Have you ever noticed that the unplanned adventures
are when you're the most alive?**

*For more on this topic, see Advanced Life Skills Syllabus Section VI:
Mysteries: Knowing What You Don't Know*

Did I Ever Tell You About...

MY UNPLANNED ODYSSEY ACROSS THE EASTERN PACIFIC?

*"Life is short, art long, opportunity fleeting,
experience treacherous, judgment difficult."*
— Hippocrates

I hired a boy with a small boat to row me out to where the *Nichlolas* was anchored. As I approached the ladder that went down from the main deck to the water of the harbor, I hailed the quarterdeck, "Ahoy! Ahoy, there! LTJG McMikle requesting permission to come aboard, sir!"

I saw two surprised faces looking down at me. "Permission granted! Can you identify yourself?"

"Yes, sir, I can." I had no change, so I asked the boy to wait, on the promise that I would give him my entire $20 if he waited for my return. He grinned broadly and gave me a fairly decent salute. I saluted the OOD, showed him my ID card, and requested permission to speak with the senior officer on duty. I found myself in the XO's stateroom. I told him my story, and he promptly issued me $300 in cash via Emergency Pay and messaged *Schofield* regarding my whereabouts. I knew that I had to start my journey right away, so I went back ashore, paid the boy, and set about chasing down my ship.

Feeling much more confident with $300 safely in my pocket, I first asked a taxi driver if he knew of an inexpensive hotel. He nodded and drove me a short distance to Nancy's New Harbor Hotel, a fairly new-looking two-story building on the shoreline of Kaoshiung harbor. The city was a major seaport, with many merchant ships anchored out at any given time. Nancy's New Harbor, I soon learned, catered to sailors, and I do mean "catered", in the literal sense. The entire staff spoke very good English, as well as other languages, and I soon discovered that Nancy's was a well-known R&R venue. My room was simple but clean: a bed, a closet, a bathroom, etc. However, the most prominent feature was a large red leather photo album that took up most of the nightstand, along with a telephone. As I soon learned, Chinese girls are among the most beautiful in the world, and there were some two dozen examples of them depicted in my album. It was a MENU! For each girl, there was a picture, a name, a dollar amount, and a number. To receive "room service", one needs only dial 3, wait for a cheerful female voice to say, "May I help you?", state your room number, and ask for so-and-so by number. In a matter of minutes, "room service" was announced with a gentle knock at the door. I will spare you from any sordid details. Suffice it to say that my time at Nancy's New Harbor Hotel probably extended a bit longer than required to get my bearings, due to the unexpected temptations that I felt to stay, at least long enough to sample several of the delightful entrees on the Menu. Besides, I immediately calculated that my $300 would rapidly disappear if I stayed much longer.

My journey to Yokosuka began when I managed to secure a ride in the back seat of a Chinese biplane, typically used for crop dusting, to Taipei, the capital of Taiwan. From Taipei, which had a substantial US presence, the American Embassy arranged my passage on the regular USAF mail plane to Kadena, Okinawa, which had an even stronger US presence; and from Okinawa, on a C-130 Air Force cargo plane, to Atsugi Naval Air Station in Japan. Atsugi was 80 miles north of Yokosuka. Finally, on the morning before I was to rendezvous with my ship in Yokosuka, my funds had dwindled to $14.25—not enough to hire a taxi for that last 80 miles. So there I was, sitting in front of the Navy Captain who was CO of Atsugi Naval Air Station, telling my sad tale with that (blank) ing conveyor motor on the floor beside me. The Captain had graciously consented to come to his office on a Sunday to hear my story. He burst out laughing when I had finished, but truly pitied me, and gave me the use of his staff car and driver to take me that last 80 miles to my ship.

So there I was, on the evening of the day before the *Schofield* was scheduled to sail back into the jaws of Hell for another month, plane-guarding for carriers of the Tonkin Gulf Yacht Club, as the ships of Yankee Station liked to call themselves. I thanked the driver as he pulled up to my ship, tied up at the pier. As I limped up the gangway with my motor firmly in hand, I clearly heard the quarterdeck bell ring, and the 1MC (loudspeaker) proclaim: "Bong-bong! Bong-bong! LTJG McMikle, returning!" Now, the practice of "bonging aboard" a person is normally something reserved for announcing the coming and going of important persons, like the skipper, or announcing the departure of a shipmate, when they leave the ship for the last time, as a sort of farewell salute. It's practically never used to announce the arrival of a lowly LTJG. But our skipper and XO both had a highly developed sense of humor.

I was still somewhat chagrined at my little welcome ceremony—especially when those words were immediately followed by: "Now hear this! LTJG McMikle, report to the XO's stateroom! ON THE DOUBLE!" And those words caused my stomach to sink.

"Enter", was the response to my knock. Sitting there were the XO, my Department Head, and the Senior Watch Officer. They wore very grim expressions, and I fully expected to hear next something like, "Do you have any last requests?"

But they let me tell my story—minus some of the more risque details about Nancy's—and in the silence that followed, I added, "But I successfully accomplished the mission assigned to me, sir.", nodding at the package conveyer motor, sitting on the XO's floor.

At this point, the XO, who was a very kind man at heart, burst out laughing, and so did the other two men. "And it's a damn good thing you did, Mr. McMikle, because that fact is gonna save your young ass from severe punishment". True. Had I been on R & R—or "shore leave", as it is known—and missed movement in a wartime scenario, my career would have been toast. But I had been following orders, and could not have possibly known that the ship would be ordered underway a day early. Therefore, all was forgiven. And I had another story to add to my already-lengthy repertoire.

Have you every followed orders or direction that went astray?
How? When?

For more on this topic, see Advanced Life Skills Syllabus Section III:
Leadership: Form Follows Function

Did I Ever Tell You About...

SOME OF THE DANGERS THAT AWAIT THE UNWARY AT SEA?

*"Real knowledge is to know
the extent of one's ignorance."*
— Confucius

The Ocean—the True Love of my life, can be at one moment as calm and gentle as a millpond, and the next—a blue-green horror from your worst nightmares, that will rip your mighty warship to pieces, without warning or remorse. We had gone from another three weeks fighting in the Vietnam Conflict to participation in *Operation Sea Spirit*, a multi-nation exercise, involving dozens of ships, which was to end in tragedy, terror, and death for many of those involved. Unbeknownst to any of the participants, this "training exercise" was to end badly—very badly. And I was there to see it all unfold, and to tell you the tale of it.

Since the conclusion of WW II, the Japanese have actually become one of our closest, most trustworthy allies. Having studied the ways of *bushido*, the samurai warriors' code of conduct, I have come to believe that this friendship and respect are the result of a warrior philosophy in which one warrior, even in defeat, acknowledges and honors the prowess of another. So it was that the Imperial Japanese Navy, which America devastated in WW II, morphed into the JDF—the Japanese Defense Forces. Please make no mistake; I believe that one of the deciding factors in winning the War in the Pacific was that we simply crushed them with superior numbers and manufacturing resources. The Japanese are highly skilled, highly disciplined, and technologically excellent; we overwhelmed them with the weight of our numbers.

Operation Sea Spirit included ships from the US, the JDF, the British, and the Aussies. We had all been antagonists fifty years earlier, but now we faced a larger, more formidable foe: Communism. The armed forces of Russia, China, North Korea, and North Vietnam were all aligned against the freedom-loving countries of the world—and constant training and practice was what helped us to keep our fighting edge. Sea Spirit was a days-long training exercise that involved multiple Anti-Submarine, Anti-Aircraft, and Surface Warfare drills of multiple types. For this particular drill, we had a veteran Japanese Defense Forces commander, who was aboard to witness the "advanced ASW technologies of the US Navy"—to wit, our new SQS-26 Sonar, ASROC missile platform, and, most importantly, our prototype, stern-firing, sound-guided torpedo system. This was one of the advanced, experimental weapons systems for which Schofield, and her sister ships of the Brooke-class DEG's, were designed.

Commander Urochi, the JDF representative, observed closely as we made our approach on one of our old diesel submarines to test our experimental torpedo, which was equipped with America's newest audio-homing guidance system. In theory, this torpedo would detect the faintest sounds made by a submerged enemy sub, home in on them through their noise signature, and explode against the sub's hull. This "enemy" sub had been ordered to be especially noisy, to provide a better target with which to impress the Japanese observer. The torpedo warhead, of course, was inert.

So it was with rapt attention, from all hands on the bridge, that we slowed to 10 knots, the range-to-target closed to 1,000 yards, and the order was given to fire. The torpedo whooshed as it emerged from our stern firing tube. Everything went perfectly...until it was noticed that the wake of our torpedo, which could be seen through binoculars, slowly formed a wide circle that—ever so slowly—passed the bearing of the target sub, and continued...right back towards our own ship.

"ALL STOP! ALL STOP, GODDAMMIT!" screamed the Skipper, at the top of his lungs. But it was too late. The torpedo had acquired our propellers, and even though we had shut down our own prop, the torpedo was equipped with a "fire-and-forget" technology that remembered the location where the sound had

last been detected. *"5…4…3…2…1. Impact!"* was heard on the 1MC, immediately followed by a loud THUD! as the dummy warhead bounced off our stern.

A long, uncomfortable silence settled over the bridge. Our Skipper slowly turned a bright shade of pink when the Japanese Commander, who had been very polite and circumspect during all of these unfolding events, managed to barely stifle his smirk as he turned, bowed to our CO, and said, *"Ah, so, Captain. Too bad you did not have those in our last War."* I had been JOOD for this incident, as well, and would have normally made the log entries that would be the official record of this incident. But this time, for reasons that everyone understood, the CO insisted on taking the logbook to his cabin and writing the official description of the incident himself.

A completely honest and plain-language entry would have read something like this: *"At 0916 hours on 26 May 1969, Schofield shot herself in the ass."* Of course, the official entry, as written by the Skipper, was far less graphic. I read it when my watch came up again that evening. The logbook had quietly been returned to the Quartermaster's table on the bridge, an hour after the CO had removed it, and the damning entry read: *"Due to serious equipment malfunction, scheduled torpedo exercise was aborted."*

And it is in such ways, my friends, that history is recorded. I was reminded of a famous anecdote from the Napoleonic Wars of 19th-century Europe. Napoleon was famous for hating bad news and had a reputation for punishing the messenger who brought it. And in the days leading up to Waterloo, when one of his generals had suffered a stinging defeat, this general sent the messenger back with this note: *"I am pleased to inform His Imperial Majesty that we are retreating in perfect order, before an enemy who is advancing in utter confusion."*

Have you experienced rewritten history?

For more on this topic, see Advanced Life Skills Syllabus Section I: Effective Human Communications

Did I Ever Tell You About...

THE TERRIBLE FINAL CHAPTER OF OPERATION SEA SPIRIT?

*"Whoever sails as master of all truth
makes his own shipwreck upon the rocks of the gods' laughter."*
— Modern paraphrase, inspired by Albert Einstein.

O*peration Sea Spirit* was slowly winding down, and we had about two days remaining when the vast multi-ship exercise came to an early, unexpected, and tragic conclusion. And, once again, *Schofield* was smack dab in the middle of the action. Every sailor knows about the story of how the *USS Frank E. Evans* (DD-754), an aging WW II Sumner-class destroyer, was literally chopped in half by a collision with the RAN *Melbourne*, a Royal Australian Navy carrier taking part in Operation Sea Spirit. But what "everyone" doesn't know is the inside story, the human story, of the men involved in that incident. But I do. I was there.

The *Schofield* was part of the anti-submarine screening formation that surrounded the *Melbourne* on that fateful night. Our screening station was located on the starboard quarter of the carrier (right rear). Once again, I was the JOOD in *Schofield*, steaming at a steady 15 knots, 1,000 yards astern. LTJG Bob Ramsey, with whom I had raised a few glasses while on liberty, was Officer of the Deck in the *Evans*, in the port bow position of the screening formation. We received orders to shift stations, and this intersection of Man and Machine brought about the death of 74 brothers-in-arms at 0403 that night. I first learned of it when CIC handed the OOD a message, on what is now a faded yellow scrap of paper, which I still have in my safe:

"Evans is in two halves.
FINEX…FINEX…FINEX"

The full story of who did what, and "Who Shot John", was to be a subject recorded on thousands of dead trees in the annals of US Naval History. The brutal truth is that "the System" killed those men. Bob Ramsey had been exhausted. He had been pushed hard to pass his OOD qualifications due to a lack of sufficient qualified watch officers on his ship.

There were two levels of "Officer of the Deck" qualifications. Independent OODs (OOD/I) were officers qualified to operate the ship when it was steaming alone. The OOD on watch exercised all the powers of the Captain, while he had the "deck and the conn", i.e., complete control of the vessel. At this time, I was a qualified OOD/I, but the requirements for being Fleet qualified, i.e., qualified to operate the ship in company with other ships, were much more demanding. An OOD/F (Fleet) officer had to be proficient in the many complex and demanding requirements of operating with other vessels of all types. These days, the issue has been addressed by creating the SWO (Surface Warfare Officer) designation, which is accompanied by the wearing of a gold pin (for officers) or a silver pin (for enlisted personnel). SWO status is an important milestone in a sailor's career. It marks that individual as competent to command in all functions, up to and including taking the ship into combat, also known as "fighting the ship".

Bob Ramsey was a fine officer; however, he was just too tired and too inexperienced to cope with the hand that was dealt to him that night. To make a long story shorter, the order to shift stations involved the *Melbourne* turning to port, to change the direction of the formation, and the other screening ships making other turns to reorient the formation to a new steaming axis. This is a common tactic in combat, but to attempt it at night, in formation with multiple other ships, is extremely hazardous, at best. It is nearly impossible to describe the confusion that comes from trying to keep track of dozens of multi-colored lights on the surface of the water, all moving in different directions at once, at almost 20 mph. Bob Ramsey lost track of which set of colored lights represented the carrier, resulting in both the *Evans* and the *Melbourne* colliding with each other. As each bridge gang observed the situation, it was too late to correct it.

The *Melbourne* struck the *Evans* at Frame 25, and the aging ship's steel girders, made fragile by nearly 30 years of bending in all directions, snapped like a dry twig. Frame 25 roughly defined the front third of the ship. It also happened to be the location of the only hatchway leading to the Forward Berthing Compartment, where all of the ship's Ensigns were asleep in their bunks. When the collision occurred, a snapped beam jammed that hatchway shut, guaranteeing a watery grave for all 74 officers and men, some two miles below the surface of the ocean. One can only imagine their frantic, final moments on the way to the bottom, upended and in the dark, as the oxygen slowly ran out, and the icy depths mercifully ended their horror when that remnant of the hull was crushed like an eggshell. Rest well, my brothers. We will all meet again, someday…

Schofield, since we were literally one of the first on the scene, was assigned to SAR—Search and Rescue—duty. One scene will be forever burned into my memory: the two ship captains, the *Melbourne's* Skipper and the Evans' CO, CDR McLemore, running to each others' arms on the flight deck of the carrier; both crying out, *"I'm sorry!"* as they embraced. Both seasoned, professional warriors. Both knowing that they were ultimately responsible. Both knowing that their careers were over. Both knowing that lives were forever changed. Both wondering how they would explain this night to their families.

As part of the SAR patched together by our CO, I saw it. It was a cacophony of search lights, sirens, shouting and crying, and helicopter blades going chewy-chewy-chewy in the coming dawn. The utter despair was a palpable thing, felt by all present, as the sun rose on that summer morning, on a glassy sea, so far away and long ago. And I cried, too, unashamedly.

A tug towed what remained of the *Evans* back to Subic Bay. We steamed back to Yankee Station and the War, accompanied by Bob Dylan wailing in concert, as we began the cycle again, bombing the hell out of the enemy. Bob Ramsey fell into a dark sea of inquiries and courts-martial, as the blame game began. The Evans incident is still studied at Annapolis to this day, but the naked truth is that no amount of training can prepare one for the inevitable cost of this game that we call "war." The simple fact is that Bob Ramsey could have been any of us. Patriots all, but wrong place, wrong time, wrong people at the controls.

And the rest is history…

Have you ever been involved in a serious accident?
How did you respond?

For more on this topic, see Advanced Life Skills Syllabus Section VII:
Is That All There Is? (Penetrating the Veil)

Did I Ever Tell You About...

WHAT'S IT'S LIKE TO BE IN A TYPHOON AT SEA?

*"In the eye of the storm, where the winds fall silent,
the soul learns that the fiercest tumult
can cradle a terrible, holy quiet."*
— *(author unknown)*

In the old days of sail, tragedies at sea were many and often. It's no exaggeration to say that those were the days of "Wooden Ships and Iron Men". But even then, it was said that until a sailor had survived his first violent storm at sea, you weren't a sailor. Well, I guess that qualifies me as a sailor, because I did exactly that. After the participants of ***Operation Sea Spirit*** had all returned to their homeports, we were assigned to Taiwan Straits patrol duty before heading back to our homeport of Long Beach, California. Taiwan and mainland China were bitter rivals. The democracy-loving followers of Chiang Kai-shek had rejected the Communist ideology of Mao Zedong. They fled to the island of Taiwan to found the Chinese Nationalist government, and Mao was their sworn enemy. The

United States, of course, became Taiwan's ally, and part of that relationship was maintaining a constant reminder of US presence in the region. So, it was that, in the remaining months of our deployment, we were detached from The Little Beavers and dispatched to sail up and down the Taiwan Strait as a symbolic defender of that country's independence from the Reds. Mother Nature had a message for all of us about who was really in charge of things…

So, it was our task to sail a long zig-zag pattern up and down the Taiwan Straits, literally "showing the flag" to Mao and his followers, as a reminder that the US really did have Taiwan's back. I was coming off morning watch when the CIC (Combat Information Center, located directly behind the bridge) received a message regarding Typhoon Elsie, a fully formed Category 4 typhoon (hurricane) bearing straight down on us. There's no such thing as calling the game due to bad weather in the Navy. It was early September, and an unusually warm summer had heated the tropical waters to a turmoil. A typhoon is essentially a giant thermal engine, a means for the ocean to release the tremendous energy accumulated by excessive warm air rising from the surface.

"NOW HEAR THIS, NOW HEAR THIS! ALL HANDS RIG AND STAND BY FOR HEAVY WEATHER. I SAY AGAIN, ALL HANDS PREPARE FOR HEAVY WEATHER!"

The storm was, quite literally, a 175-mph monster from which there was no escape. The size of Elsie was enormous, almost 250 miles across, and the eye of the storm was forecast to run right smack through the middle of our duty station. The storm's diameter would easily swallow the entire Taiwan Straits, so there was, literally, nowhere to run. And Elsie would be right on top of us in about 24 hours. Waterspouts, which are tornadoes over the ocean, were touching down in advance of the storm's path. We were equipped with a special height-finding radar (the SPA-52) that detected one such waterspout, approximately 15 miles distant. I watched the radar screen in fascination, unable to tear my eyes away, even though I was just off watch, tired, and hungry. Being on a ship at sea is exhausting enough under normal conditions; the body constantly pushes back, even in one's sleep, against the ship's ever-shifting center of gravity. There was an eerie silence as the entire bridge watch team listened to the distant rumbling of thunderstorms. I stepped out on the starboard bridge wing and trained my binoculars on the bearing where the radar showed the typhoon to be located…and suddenly, there it was: a long, dark funnel cloud that reminded me of that famous scene from *The Wizard of Oz*.

The monster reached down from a flat, dark cloud bank that hid the approach of Elsie, some 80-miles behind it. I stood, mesmerized at the sight, only to be jarred back to reality by the OOD barking out: *"LEFT STANDARD RUD-*

DER, STEER COURSE 270! ENGINES AHEAD FULL, MAKE TURNS FOR 20 KNOTS!"

Promptly followed by the equally excited responses, *"Aye, aye, sir, my rudder is left standard, making my course 270!"*

"Engines ahead full, make turns for 20 knots, aye sir!", coming from the helm and lee helm, respectively. Both men were gripping their controls nervously. And it was no wonder. The giant funnel cloud was bearing down on us at frightening speed. The OOD (Officer of the Deck) had correctly followed standard procedure by, after plotting the course that the typhoon was traveling, increasing speed and turning 90 degrees away from that axis. But everyone who could see it watched in fascination as the storm, almost as if deliberately steered by some malignant weather-demon, slowly turned course to intercept us.

"CAPTAIN TO THE BRIDGE!" The Skipper appeared on the bridge, looking disheveled and bleary-eyed.

"Where away, Mr. Thomas?" the CO asked of the OOD.

"Dead astern, Captain. I just turned away from its plot, but it seems to have also changed to follow us". LT Andy Thomas, a seasoned, very competent deck officer, appeared pale and shaken as he stared at the funnel from the starboard bridge wing. The Skipper pointed his own binoculars at the grim apparition that, as illogical as it sounds, did indeed seem to be intent on hitting us! We finally evaded the grim giant and turned our attention back to its Mother, Typhoon Elsie. As we turned back to base course, we crossed over what had been the wake of the waterspout…and suddenly, it was raining fish! The evil grey giant had acted like a giant vacuum cleaner, sucking up thousands of smaller fish and giant chunks of what must have been sharks and other marine creatures. Although no one was hungry at the moment, the OOD sent a detail out on the main deck to gather up as many of the wriggling critters as possible…on the prospect of having fresh fish to eat after we got clear of Elsie.

Now, I have been airsick, trainsick, and sick on roller coasters; but, for some odd reason, I have never been seasick—nor was I now. The heaving seas had a bad effect on most everyone else, however. A device called a *"clinometer"* hung on a beam over the ship's wheel; its function was to show the degrees to port or starboard of horizontal, so measuring how far the ship was heeled over. Normal inclination in normal, gently rolling seas was 5-10 degrees, back and forth. *Schofield* was designed, by virtue of her SQS-26 experimental sonar dome, a bulbous protrusion from her underwater bow that was flooded with some 40 tons of seawater. This huge mass acted as a counterweight at one end of a pendulum, and so (theoretically) could recover from an 80-degree roll, nearly horizontal. No one had yet tested that design feature, but then no sane sailor ever wanted to! World War II-era destroyers had a capsize point of nearly 60 degrees to port or starboard.

But they did not have our experimental sonar. I will tell you frankly, dear readers, that to this day, the next 24 hours were the most terrifying of my young life, thus far…

There was one moment about which I still have nightmares. We were enduring the second half of the storm, but Mother Nature was saving the worst for last—Twin 1200-psi pressure-fired boilers engines powered *Schofield*. The old standard was a series of 600-psi boilers; our turbines were another experimental feature of the *Brooke-class* frigates… and these were especially vulnerable to salt water being sucked down the vents, thus causing the boilers to lose fires…and that was incredibly dangerous to the ship's survival. In a storm like Elsie, STOP (Standard Operating Procedure) was to keep the storm on your ship's starboard quarter (rear right side). As the storm grew nearer and the rolls averaged 25-30 degrees, not all deck-qualified officers were able to stand quarterdeck watch: Even the Captain, a seasoned and fully qualified officer, was strapped, moaning, into his bunk by his orderlies. We each stood for 3 hours in rotation; that was about the amount each of us could stand without a break. I say "stand, but the correct term might be "strung", because every member of the minimal bridge crew had to be strapped to the stanchions (vertical steel poles) which ran from deck to beams overhead. The most dreaded part of the process was the time when we had to relieve the watch, because we literally had to crab-crawl to our watch station and hang on for dear life until the straps were removed from one officer and attached to the next. When we took stock after passing through the other half of Elsie's record-breaking girth, not a man of the crew was without multiple bruises and contusions. At one point, although there were no "black box" equivalents on US Navy ships back then, I would swear that I saw the clinometer reach an unheard-of 50 degrees — over halfway to horizontal! Our worst casualty occurred when a large watertight steel hatchway door broke loose from its latches and slammed shut on a sailor's hand, severing several fingers. This poor man had to be airlifted off to a Naval medical facility as soon as we were clear of the storm; his war was over, and we never saw him again…

But back to that nightmare moment. We were enduring the last of Elsie, and Lt. Thomas and I drew the Mid-0300 shift. And Mother Nature threw one of her curveballs at yours truly; see if you can picture this. Scientists call them *"rogue waves"*; I call them Sea Demons. A hugely terrifying wave came at us from the port quarter (left rear); it flipped the ship to one side, and try as we might, the ship jerked violently, like a bone being shaken by a giant pit bull. Water came pouring across the engine room intake vents…and moments later, the engine room's frantic message sent chills up everyone's spine: *"BRIDGE, ENGINE ROOM! LOST FIRES, LOST FIRES IN PORT BOILER!"*

"HELM, STEER 20 DEGREES TO PORT! STARBOARD ENGINE,

FLANK SPEED! I SAY AGAIN, FLANK SPEED!"

While the helm and lee helm barked their responses, still tethered to my stanchion, I signaled the BMOW to loosen my safety lines, then stepped out onto the starboard bridge wing, and looked astern…and up!…only to see the Behemoth, the subject of years of future nightmares, bearing down on us like a huge, green monster from the depths of Hell. The ship was surfing down a gigantic wave. The masthead height (top of the mast) of the *Brooke-class* frigates was just over 100 feet. The crest of this wave towered at least another masthead length over that! If we were to lose power in the starboard boiler, the ship would be unable to hold course, and we would broach (turn sideways) and roll over into a watery tomb.

I prayed loudly with every fiber of my being to Almighty God and His son, Jesus Christ, and begged Him to be merciful and restrain this terrible sea.

To this day, I KNOW that He heard my prayer, for in the next moment the 1MC blared, **BRIDGE, ENGINE ROOM! FIRES RE-LIT IN PORT BOILER!** Quickly followed with, "**HELMSMAN, RETURN TO BASE COURSE 270 DEGREES! ALL ENGINES AHEAD FULL!**" I nearly collapsed against my straps as the waves of relief swept over every man on the bridge. They all stared at us as if we were Joan of Arc and her angels.

A few days later, after the storm was gone further West, and we were still licking our wounds, Smitty (Quartermaster Second Class Smith), who had been my helmsman during that awful moment, came up to me and said, "*Mr. McMikle, I just gotta tell you…*" he looked down. He stammered, "*Well, sir, I think you and Mr. Thomas saved everybody's lives back there, sir. If you hadn't done what you did, exactly when you did it, we'd all be at the bottom.*"

"*No, Smitty. Thanks, but it was God who saved us. I just asked Him for help*".

He shook my hand, saluted, and walked away.

Have you ever felt death's wings brush over you?
How did you react?

For more on this topic, see Advanced Life Skills Syllabus Section VII:
Is That All There Is? (Penetrating the Veil)

Did I Ever Tell You About...

HOW I GOT MARRIED (THE FIRST TIME)?

*"Thrice happy and more are they,
whom an unbroken bond holds fast."*
— *Horace, Carmina*

We steamed back into Long Beach, California, that following September, which was our newly assigned home port. The end of my two-year active-duty obligation as a Reservist was approaching, and the trauma I had experienced during my first deployment had led me to delay applying to "go Regular", i.e., switch from being a Reservist, doing monthly weekend training drills and a two-week active duty stint every year, to be a full-time Navy officer. Besides, something else got in the way. I fell in love with a girl I met, and got married.

Let's call her "Cindy" to preserve her privacy, since she's still alive and well, and the mother of my adult daughter. I had some time on my hands for the first time in months, so I went to social events in the local community. At a dance at the Officer's Club on base, I met a short, cute, blue-eyed blonde girl who was was in her final internship as a physical therapist at a local hospital. We danced, laughed, and had a few drinks before exchanging phone numbers. I had rented a simple apartment in town, just for a change of pace, and set about planning the next steps I would take in my life. Cindy and I discovered that we shared a keen interest in camping and "exploring" the great outdoors—and Southern California had an abundance of interesting venues for those activities. Cindy had a close friend and co-worker named Magdalena—"Maggie", so I fixed her up with a fellow officer from the ship, Bill. All four of us ended up on a weekend camping trip to the Anzio-Berrega Desert, in the mountainous area just 50 miles east of the coast. We had rented tents from the base Welfare and Recreation office, and found what we thought was a remote area to camp for the weekend. We stayed up late around our campfire, toasted marshmallows, sang and drank too much wine, and fell asleep.

We suddenly awoke to the roar of many engines on both sides of our campground. I scrambled to my feet and looked outside the tent. There were dozens of "dune-buggies"—chopped-down cars modified with extra-wide tires and rear-mounted engines, plus multiple dirt bikes—rushing past our campsite on both sides. We had unknowingly camped in the middle of a popular local dirt-track rally, and they were having their monthly *"Gymkana"*. Maggie and Bill emerged from their tent, and we all stood and watched in stupefied wonder as some 40-50 smoke-spewing vehicles sped past our campsite. The rest of the weekend went quite well, however, and both Cindy and Maggie bonded well. Over the following weeks, Cindy and I became fast friends, and we developed a deeper connection beyond just friendship.

We made a promise to each other, though, to save actual intercourse for our wedding night. We had both been intimate with lovers prior. Cindy warmed to the idea when I suggested being celibate until after the vows were exchanged. I remember how my heart was pounding when I literally took a knee and asked her. She found my "traditional" ways to be "sweet", but I was just doing what I felt was the honorable way to do things. I took the opportunity to relate to Cindy the story of Engine-Daddy and the licorice whips, and how he had impressed me with how vital honor was to a man. Cindy thought this was good, as well. Besides, I thought we were a perfect match. But that's another story; stay tuned.

We were married near Cindy's parents' home—Aurora, Colorado, at the foot of the mighty Rocky Mountains. My mom and dad flew out there for the ceremony. Cindy had a large extended family, and I had just my parents, so it made sense logistically. Besides, I had always had a yearning for the "High Lonesome", and during all my many criss-crossings of the country in the back of the Gronk, I had always enjoyed their majestic splendor more than any other part of the country—except the ocean, of course. After some indecision and a couple of false starts, we finally settled in Cheyenne, Wyoming. And the Navy was put on the back burner, as I decided not to resume active duty, but to remain a Reservist and complete my 20 years in that capacity. This was a strategic error, one that I have regretted many times since.

"Aunt Dotty", as she liked to be called, was my grandmother's sister. She had been afflicted with polio at an early age, never married, and doted on me as if I were her own son. She had gone to work, during WW II, for the OSS—the government's secret spy agency. It was re-named the CIA in 1947. Aunt Dottie had served as the Executive Secretary to the Director for over 30 years, spanning several administrations. The bottom line was that she had left me 885 shares of Con Edison stock, worth approximately $760,000. I flew to Washington, met with the estate attorneys, and performed all the necessary duties to settle the estate. I was never that close to Aunt Dottie, but I thanked God for this windfall. It all but guaranteed our financial success. The first thing we did was go house-hunting in Cheyenne itself.

We were both giddy with success and went on a shopping spree. After renting a tiny apartment as a base camp, we went house hunting. Cindy traded in her red Camaro for a bright yellow Jeep Commando, and I bought a slightly used powder-blue Mercedes-Benz 230 with only 2,000 miles on the odometer; it may as well have been a new car. I had a flashback to that dusty day in Kingsville, long ago and far away, when I saw that ten-dollar bill there in the street, and came to my senses. I took what remained after all our purchases, paid off Aunt Dotty's debts (about $12,000), and bought 100-oz silver bars. This turned out to be a lifesaver some years later.

But back to how we started out...

Have you ever experienced an abrupt change in your priorities? How did you respond, and why?

For more on this topic, see Advanced Life Skills Syllabus Section IV: Universal Laws, Hiding in Plain Sight

Did I Ever Tell You About...

THAT I ONCE LIVED IN A GLASS HOUSE?

"Who that hath an hed of verre,
Fro cast of stones war hym in the werre,"
— *Geoffrey Chaucer*

After starting life in Cheyenne in that diminutive apartment, Cindy and I eventually went house-hunting after settling into our jobs. I have always been known for favoring the unusual things in life, and this time was no exception. In June of that year, we found a listing in the local paper for "The Bottle House". This was an item of gossip among the local population. There was a gentleman named J.H. Widholm who retired from a career as a mortician's supply salesman.

Over his career, he collected and saved all the empty bottles of embalming fluid (formaldehyde) that he sold to the various funeral homes in Wyoming and Northern Colorado that he serviced. His friends thought he was nuts—and perhaps he was—but by the time he retired, he had a collection of over 30,000 empty embalming fluid bottles, all of uniform size and shape. Since it takes about 3 bottles of fluid to embalm the average adult, his collection represented some 10,000 dead people. He then set about to find a special cement mix that would bind to the bottles, and set about building a house—designed to look like a small castle, with conical towers. It was designed like a dumb-bell in cross-section; two large round sections, one with the living room/dining area and one with bedroom/bath/closets on the other, connected by a rectangular center section with kitchen and fireplace. We actually cooked over that fireplace, like they did in medieval castles. The bottles were set so that the butt-ends—the thickest part—faced outward. With the caps firmly screwed on, they trapped dead air that was warmed by the sun, so made for perfect insulation. Dug into the hillside at the rear of the house was an extra-large garage and storage area. The house sat on 8 acres of land, about 20 miles Northwest of Cheyenne. The parcel was at the 8,000 ft. level, serviced by electrical power, a well, and a gravel road. Elk, deer, and other wild game were around the area in abundance. For Cindy and me, it was love at first sight! We paid $12,500 for the property and proceeded to settle into our new dream home, surrounded by nature, crisp mountain air, brilliant sunshine, and the joy of rural home ownership.

This was the beginning of my "Jeremiah Johnson" period; I grew a beard, and harvested deer and rabbits from the surrounding forests. Cheyenne's main water source, Granite Reservoir, was a short walk down the mountain, and was teeming with beautiful Rocky Mountain trout, which Cindy and I caught on cheese balls and pan-fried with hush puppies, butter and lemon, over an open fire. I have fine memories of dining on slow-roasted venison haunch, cooked rotisserie-style in our fireplace. I became an excellent shot with hunting bow and arrow, and often harvested our dinner Indian-style. We were in Heaven! The satisfaction of my happy days on the farm returned for a time. When Cindy's birthday rolled around, I surprised her with an AKC-registered English Sheepdog puppy. We named him "Sir Scoby Snowboots" (Scoby), and that adorable little furball rounded out our little family…for the present, at least. He eventually tangled with a skunk, and I used an old trick I had learned with our beagles on the farm: soak the dog's fur in tomato juice. Poor Scoby looked like he'd been hit by a truck, but he was allowed back in the house after his tomato shampoo.

But we were about to get an education in that old real estate maxim: "Location, location, location", as in: SEASONS CHANGE. We had purchased the Bottle House in Summer, when the weather was gorgeous; it was a different thing altogether in the depths of a brutal Wyoming Winter. The well froze up, and we literally had to melt ice on the stove to have water. The gravel road to Cheyenne sometimes snowed over to depth of 2-3 feet, and even our trusty Jeep, fitted with snow chains, struggled to make it through on some days. We used to huddle around the huge fireplace in the evenings, which would accommodate 4 ft. long split logs, sip hot chocolate with crème de menthe, and wonder what we had been thinking…

During that time, Cindy and I both managed to do well at our respective jobs, and both achieved raises and promotions. Life was good, but after a month or too enduring an hour-long commute down the mountain to our jobs in town became just too much. So, we got a small apartment in Cheyenne, and only went to the cabin on weekends. To this day, the "Bottle House" is a local legend, and it still holds fond memories surrounding my Jeremiah Johnson period.

Have you ever experienced buyer's remorse?
What did you learn from it?

For more on this topic, see Advanced Life Skills Syllabus Section V:
Rules of Success to Adopt Before Your 20's

Did I Ever Tell You About...

MY EARLY ADVENTURES IN THE (NEW) WILD, WILD WEST?

"Your joy is your sorrow unmasked.
And the selfsame well from which
your laughter rises was oftentimes filled with your tears."
— *Kahlil Gibran*

From the vantage point of age, I should have signed on for full-time Active-Duty Service in the US Navy, completed my 20 years, and then gone on to something else. As it was, God had other plans for me, and I have since learned to trust Him. God answers all prayers—even if the answer is sometimes "NO". I was in love with the idea of being in love, a married man with a family to build. Cindi was hired as a physical therapist for the local school district, and I accepted a position as a Forensic Technician with the Wyoming Attorney General's Office. They were both good, solid jobs that paid decent salaries for the times. We worked hard, saved our money, and were soon able to buy the "bottle house" on 8 acres of land, a few miles West of Cheyenne without touching the inheritance that Aunt Dotty had left me. Our cabin was at the 8,000-ft level, and our backyard was literally part of the elk migration trail. Cindi and I were both lovers of the outdoors, and it was a joy to sit on our back porch and watch the elk and deer grazing on our property. We spent every weekend exploring the mountains and forests around Cheyenne, which stood at the base of the Front Range. I decided to enroll in the MBA program at the University of Wyoming, where I was able to pursue a business degree and become a better breadwinner. But Life, my friends, has a way of being unpredictable. Cindi confronted me one morning at breakfast with the simple words, "I'm pregnant".

"HOW CAN YOU BE PREGNANT?" I gasped, spewing coffee on my plate.

Cindi and I had often discussed the idea of children, and we had both agreed to wait until we had built up enough savings and other resources to raise our first child comfortably. We had agreed to wait at least two years, just as "us". To ensure this, she had been taking the new birth control pill, "Enovid". Somehow, however, she had managed to be impregnated, anyway. We read the instructions on the box: "…proven to be 95% effective in preventing unwanted pregnancies".

"Welcome to the 5%", mumbled Cindi. I remained in a state of shock, but Cindi started warming to the idea of motherhood, and I sensed that she was secretly glad about our little "whoops".

As she progressed, her morning sickness became overwhelming. Some days, she was so sick that she could barely get out of bed, let alone fulfill a work day in town. So, one day when I came in the door, she was sitting in front of the fireplace with a cat-like grin on her cute face. "Oh, honey, I have the most wonderful drug that my doctor prescribed for my sickness. Look here!"

And she tossed me the bottle. "Thalidomide", I read. "Does it work?" I asked.

"Oh, it's wonderful! I started taking it this morning and I feel lots better already". Everything went well after that, or so it seemed. With the help of the new miracle drug, Cindi was able to get through a regular day, working with children with disabilities at the school clinic. I was coming to grips with the idea of being a father, and was actually looking forward to it. I had received a promotion and raise at work, as my supervisors had recognized that I had nearly mastered fingerprint technology, blood-spatter analysis, and other aspects of crime-scene investigation in my first year on the job. Cindi was in her ninth month, and the poor woman was hugely with child.

"It's gotta be a boy", said her father, Bob. And he told me that women near full term acquire strange cravings, and to this day I remember coming into the kitchen after hearing noises in the middle of the night, only to find Cindy hunched over a bowl of something that looked—and smelled—disgusting. When I asked, she responded, "Oh, it's sardines and chocolate syrup with pickle relish. Marvelous! Want some?"

I shook my head and stumbled back to bed.

And as the days passed and her due date approached, her doctor prescribed long walks in the evening. And so, sure enough, it was during one of those walks that Cindi gasped, held her swollen abdomen with both hands, looked at me, and whispered, "I think he's coming".

At roughly 1:00 am that morning, I stood beside Cindi in the delivery room and held her hand as she gave birth to our son, Derek. I was never prouder than at that moment. There is something absolutely awe-inspiring about being present at the birth of your son. I had never known such utter joy. But the staff shooed me out of the room, and I jabbered with her parents in the Waiting Room while mother and child got cleaned up. A half-hour passed, and then another. I was ready to go back in and find out the reason for the delay when the doctor appeared and asked us all to sit down. I will never forget the grim look on his face, and that old feeling of foreboding tingling down my spine…

"Mr. McMikle, I'm afraid I have some unpleasant news. Your wife is doing fine, but your son was born with some abnormalities." That tingling turned to cold dread. "Well, his heart valves are virtually in the wrong positions, and his heart is literally pumping against itself. He's getting very little actual blood supply to his brain and other organs. He's in intensive care at the moment…"

We found out later that Thalidomide, the drug that Cindi had used, was suspected to have caused Derek's congenital disability. Too late to be of any help to him.

That night did not end well. They finally let us see Derek when the sun was coming up. He couldn't be let out of the incubator. And as Cindi's parents and I leaned in closer, through the glass we saw that our little boy was a faint bluish-white all over, and lacked even the strength to cry. All of us did enough of that for him.

My brave little boy, Derek William McMikle, lived for 18 months. We were able to take him home for brief periods and go through the motions of child-rearing, but we were only waiting for him to gain enough weight to attempt corrective heart surgery. I have pictures of one of the few times that he smiled. He must have been in constant pain, all the time.

Derek's condition was a medical curiosity, so much so that Johns Hopkins University sent a team of specialists to witness it and assist with the surgery. Cindi and I held each other as we watched them wheel our little man into that pale green room. It was the last time we ever saw him alive. Today, a plain gravestone stands in the Ft Carson, Colorado, military cemetery. It reads, *"Derek William McMikle, son of LT Steven and Mrs. Cindi McMikle, OCT 1972"*. And a little piece of my heart is buried there with him.

Once we had buried Derek, Cindi and I sat down at the table and had a long talk. We agreed to give ourselves time to heal before attempting to have another child. I poured myself into my graduate school studies and was able to graduate with my Master of Business Administration degree from the University of Wyoming in May 1975. I had built a decent reputation with the Attorney General's Office. When word of my MBA became known, I received a job offer from the Wyoming State Auditor's Office to serve as a Senior Financial Systems Analyst. This position came with a $12,000 salary increase, my own office, and a heap of possibilities. Over the next decade, I managed to distinguish myself at the Wyoming Auditor's Office. The six-inch-thick procedures manual for the Wyoming Uniform Accounting System remained the Bible for all things financial, and the series of training courses that I authored for each type of fiscal employee.

I stayed in Cheyenne for a total of 15 years, and although it is only one of many places where I have hung my hat, I have always considered it "home". Maybe it has something to do with Derek, but I have considered my "roots" to be nestled there, at the base of the Rockies. Cindi and I had our disagreements, and I became a victim of "Seven-Year Itch". Suffice it to say that we parted on good terms. Out of respect for both my daughter and my ex-wife, I will simply say that our lives went in different directions.

Imagine how different your life would become if you were told that you would die within a year? How would you live?

For more on this topic, see Advanced Life Skills Syllabus Section V: Rules of Success to Adopt Before Your 20's

Did I Ever Tell You About...

THAT I WAS ONCE A PROFESSIONAL ASTROLOGER?

"The stars are like letters that inscribe themselves at every moment in the sky. Everything in the world is full of signs. All events are coordinated. All things depend on each other. Everything breathes together."
— *Plotinus*

As you can tell by now, I have always been attracted to things mystical, unusual, and bizarre. My UW advisor conferred, and agreed that my Master's Thesis topic would be a statistical exercise. I had always, up to that point, been of the opinion that "astrology", at least the popular newspaper variety, was absolute hocus-pocus junk, and perhaps even forbidden by Scripture.

As I was to discover in the coming weeks, it is an ancient wisdom based on simple observation: people noticed that men and women born at certain times of the year tended to have similar basic characteristics. We can trace the earliest references of Western astrology to ancient Mesopotamia, to the great Babylonian civilizations in the "Land Between the Rivers". They studied the stars and planets to determine the destinies of kings and noblemen. (Oriental cultures produced their own versions, but they were based on the same principles). These original seekers of the truth, were called the "magi".

The concept that this was somehow "evil", I believe, sprang from several, short Scriptural passages, one of which is "Thou shalt not suffer a witch to live", which appears in Exodus 22:18. But I have since learned that, like so many other Scriptural passages which are eagerly seized upon by over-enthusiastic zealots, is based upon total mis-interpretations of Scriptural wisdom. All of these Biblical admonishments forbid divination, i.e., "fortune-telling"; accurate mathematical astrology does not pretend to predict the future. Instead, genuine astrology defines and identifies an individual subject's "toolbox"; the strengths and weakness in a person's natal chart. One could potentially predict a person's future by identifying strong talents in fields such as medicine, law, and business acumen. But this in no way "fortune-telling" or devination. When properly applied, genuine astrology has successfully predicted human successes—or failures—for millions of people across time and space.

Bottom Line: far from being forbidden, scientific astrology is given to us, by the Creator, to understand ourselves better. From this process, something else is revealed about human nature: people in power tend to distrust, and disapprove of immediately anything that makes individuals less dependent on their leaders and other entities that have control over the masses.

A striking example of this phenomenon, historically, is found in the infamous "witch-burnings" of Europe in the 15th through the 18th centuries. And who were these "witches" who were sought out to endure a hideous death in the flames? They were the mid-wives, the masters of herbal cures, and time-tested natural "cures".

"Physiks", as they called medical doctors then, were expensive. The common folk turned to the mid-wives for cheap cures and for assisting mothers to give birth. The mid-wives were cutting into the "physiks" income. So, it was these men who led the charge against "witches". Reminds us of how it works today…

Anyway, the circumstances that launched me into the World of Professional Astrology came about when the time came for me to submit my Master's Degree Thesis for review. I was a straight- "A" student, and my faculty advisor was quite fond of me, so we met to choose a topic. My MBA minor was Statistics, so I decided to prove the notion that astrology was nothing more than a phony entertainment venue for the ignorant masses. This was 1975, and the question, "What's your sign?" was in vogue. My advisor approved this topic, which I eagerly seized upon. The aim was to conduct a random sample of 100 fellow students and have them answer a set of questions based on whether their Natal Chart (i.e., "horoscope") accurately reflected what their birth information indicated "the stars" would suggest. The first step in doing this was to become knowledgeable.

To my surprise, there was actually an organization called the American Federation of Astrologers, and I signed up to take their courses and become a "certified" astrologer. To my even greater surprise, I learned that REAL astrology was, in fact, applied spherical trigonometry. This was a piece of cake for me, because I was already a qualified navigator, and spherical trig was a skill-set that navigators used daily. So, in no time, I knew how to cast someone's chart. I was fascinated to discover that a person's Sun sign was only ONE of hundreds of independent variables in a person's chart. There are planetary placements, aspects, houses, and many other factors. To cast an accurate chart, the astrologer needed time/place/date of the subject's birth. Even then, someone born in the same hospital, at the same time of day, would turn out differently due to environmental factors.

For example, suppose two newborn baby boys, side by side, both had all the variables required for being a good surgeon. The son of wealthy family might send him to Harvard, where, sure enough, he would become a renowned surgeon. The son of a poorer family might grow up to be an excellent butcher. Same variables, different upbringing.

When I knew what to expect from each sample subject, having cast their natal charts, the final results, to my everlasting surprise, concluded that true, scientific astrology had a 93% confidence level of accuracy! My counselor was equally surprised, and insisted on researching my results, but in the end, he was also convinced.

I saw an opportunity to make some money, so…Cheyenne Astrology Services was born. Since casting a chart by hand took at least an hour, I sped up the process by automating it with a simple computer program, written using two long-extinct programming languages, FORTRAN and COBOL, and borrowing a little downtime on employer's IBM 360 computer, an actual dinosaur by today's standards. Using these tools, I was able to process a single chart in under three minutes. I then took some of my cash reserves to invest in a little advertising and marketing. In no time at all, hundreds of envelopes, each containing $5, were arriving at Cheyenne Airport. Soon, there were so many addressed to my little P.O Box, that instead of a small space stuffed with envelopes, there was a card advising me to drive around to the loading dock, where a large canvas bag was used to contain that day's mail. I had found a gold mine!

To make a long story short, my Cheyenne Astrology Services brand grew a global audience. I even had a 60-year-old Danish millionaire industrialist fly me to Copenhagen (First Class, no less!) where I performed a synastry reading (compatibility study) for him and his 18-year-old girlfriend, who was more like a Barbie doll than a real woman. Total fee for the weekend: $3,500. Not bad for a weekend's work, eh? (Of course, I told him that his proposed partner was a match made in Heaven!). After a year or so, I had accumulated enough envelopes to build a substantial bank account balance, to the point where I was able to purchase a four-unit apartment building. I eventually stopped pursuing the business as aggressively, but I still cast the occasional natal chart to this day. I have found them to be very useful when meeting a new person with whom you might be more closely associated.

Have you ever had a strong belief that was proven wrong?
How did you respond?

For more on this topic, see Advanced Life Skills Syllabus Section V:
Rules of Success to Adopt Before Your 20's

Did I Ever Tell You About...

I WAS A FAIR BAGPIPER?

*"The piper loud and louder blew,
The dancers quick and quicker flew."*
— Robert Burns

It was also about this time, fueled no doubt by the new insights that I had gained about diverse personalities, that I developed an interest in my own roots. Armed with what I already knew about heraldry and geneology, I began researching my family tree way beyond William Brown (my great-great-great-great-great grandfather on mom's side). Since I knew my biological father only by his reputation, I chose to ignore that portion of heritage, and include my step-father's MacLachlan/McMikle forebears. My Grand-dad had always said we were of Scottish origin—on both his side and on my step-father's. I discovered that my oldest directly traceable ancestors were of the Clan Stewart of Appin, who flourished during the mid-thirteenth century in the Western Highlands of Scotland. People constantly mispronounce my name as "Mick-Mickle" or variations thereof. Actually, one of the original spellings (in Scots Gaelic) is Mac Meikle; it was the Irish priests who started copying the spelling of the Archangel Michael's name for ours; the "Mac/Mc" means "son of", and is the equivalent in Irish Gaelic of the "O'-", meaning "of"; hence "O' Reilly, O'Connell", etc.

Anyway, applying my natural propensity for music, I began taking bagpipe lessons from my neighbor in Cheyenne, retired Air Force Technical Sergeant George Lucas, who had for some years served as Pipe-Major for the Air Force Pipe Band. George was a Master Piper, having studied since he was a boy. He could easily play the incredibly difficult classical bagpipe music known as *Piobaireachd* pronounced "*pee-brock*"; I was indeed fortunate to have met up with him. After a year or two, George and I began playing for weddings and funerals, and we actually had a nice side-gig going on which made a "wee bit o' sporran stuffer" as George called it. I of course acquired the full-dress regalia of the Stewart of Appin clan, and played the pipes for many years afterward. I eventually competed at the 1979 Rocky Mountain Highland Games in Denver. I did not place in the Bagpipe competition, but came in second in the Caber Toss, which is roughly equivalent to tossing a telephone pole so that it flips and lands some distance away.

Roving bands of Scots would have a Caber-Man to create temporary bridges across the many "burns" (brooks) that run through the Highlands. I never attained anything approaching George's skill, but I played the *Ciol Mor* ("Great Highland Music") for some thirty years afterward. It touched something deep within my soul. The English, in their many battles to suppress the troublesome Scots, finally classified the bagpipes as a weapon of war, and forbade their practice. They may have well enacted a tax on breathing.

The Great Highland Pipes, when played with their full vigor, are said to create vibrations in the very bone marrow of the enemy, inducing terror in them, and spurring on the fearless Scots.

Early one beautiful Wyoming morning, on an impulse, I drove West out I-80 to Vedauwoo, an ancient Native American (Arapahoe) sacred stand of red rocks overlooking the highway in the valley below. I began to play, a slow dirge at first, then a march, and finally, the little I had picked up from George of the incredible *Piobareachd*.

After fifteen minutes or so, I stopped for breath; the canyon walls still echoed with the fading notes of *Lament for Mary McLeod*. After an eerie silence, I heard faint cheering and clapping from the Interstate below; these were two lines of cars and trucks pulled over, and I was being applauded by some dozen total strangers who, for a brief moment, had stopped to share my reverie. I was humbled but proud, and in that brief moment, I was transported back to my grandpa's Highland roots, so long ago and far away...

Think about how vibration affects us.
The rythms of the world can be felt if you listen.

For more on this topic, see Advanced Life Skills Syllabus Section VII:
Is That All There Is? (Penetrating the Veil)

Did I Ever Tell You About...
ISHMAEL'S VENGEANCE ON THE WORLD?

"Evil rarely knocks at the front door; it slips in smiling, like a Trojan horse already waiting in your heart." –unknown

Is there a cultural genome for Evil? If so, it must truly be found somewhere within the ethnic Bedouin Arab ancestry, because the most toxic, brutal, and predatory belief system in the world today was spawned therein. I'm speaking, of course, of Radical Islamist Jihad, and the Shariya Law precepts that support and justify it. Simply put, in the Garden of Earth's children, Islam does not play well with others. I personally believe that the root of all this animosity toward Judeo-Christian culture, very simply, is an attitude of "We was robbed". When Ishmael, the first-born son of Abram (Abraham) was denied his father's birthright (because he was half-Arab) s in favor of Isaac, the second-born, this millennia-old seed of resentment has flowered into what I call "Ishmael's Vengeance on the World"...Radical Islamist Jihad.

Many will wince when they read these words, and cry "ISLAMOPHOBIA"! Well, if the term means "fear of Islam"—which it literally does—then WE ALL SHOULD BE AFRAID... *very afraid*. The fact that merely writing these words makes me eligible for a *fatwa*—theological sentence of death, ordered by some *mullah*, at the hands of a True Believer—should be sufficient proof of my thesis. Of all the world's major belief systems: Judeo-Christianity, Buddhism, Hinduism, Taoism, etc., only JIHADIST ISLAM (loosely translated, jihad means "struggle" in Arabic) requires the believer to conquer, enslave, tax, convert, or kill any which do not submit to the will of Allah. And it is not enough to enforce this brutal theocracy within one's borders; it requires aggressive expansion outward to other countries. In that sense, Jihadism is very much like a malignant cancer. It penetrates new host countries like the parasite it is, never to assimilate but to infest, grow, and use the liberal laws of Western countries to expand, multiply, and eventually, to culturally and politically devour the host. Sadly, as I watch newsreels of some of the great European cities I have known and loved, liberal policies implemented by moronic leaders are converting the very foundations of Western Civilization into a Jihadist cesspool.

Muhammad is literally wreaking his vengeance on the Crusaders who attempted to cleanse the Holy Land, nearly a millennium ago. When confronted with incidents of brutal "honor killings" and other murderous events, a common protest is that "Islam is a Religion of Peace, a religion of Peace!". But the devil is, literally, in the details: under the precepts of the **Qur'an, there can be no real "peace" until all have submitted to Allah!** So, when a Jihadist protests with a straight face that his actions are peaceful, he means *peace on Islam's terms!* In Arabic, *islam* is a verb which means "to submit", i.e., to the will of Allah; a muslim then becomes one who submits (to the will of Allah). Put another way, "if you don't believe in god as I do, you must be 'converted' by force". And as a non-believer (*kafiri*) , you are sub-human.

The story of how and why this one belief system acquired so much *anger* is found in ancient Scripture; specifically, Genesis 16. Now, Jews, Christians, and Muslims are all "People of the Book", i.e., believers in the first five books of the Bible and inheritors of the of Abrahamic Covenant. This bond goes back millennia, as far as the sons of Noah: Shem, Ham, and Japheth. Tradition holds that Ham went South and populated Africa, Japheth went North and founded the Caucasian nations, and Shem stuck around the Middle East. The connection appears in the term "Semitic", an ethnic group to which belong the nations around Arabia, Egypt, Israel, Jordan, Yemen, Iraq, Syria, etc. The skin coloration of this group is termed "high yellow", and includes all of the Middle-Eastern peoples. As you might now, skin coloration is a matter of climate. Hotter climates produce darker skin due to the body's production of *melanin* to protect the lower dermal layers from damage due to ultraviolet eradiation from the sun. With exceptions, the further north you live, the paler your skin.

There was another tradition that set the table for the present-day situation:

primogeniture. This is the cultural practice of making the first-born male child of a man's house the sole heir, and inheritor, of the father's goods, power, and rank among the tribe or clan. The first-born was accorded special privileges and rank, and his younger brothers were provided for at the first-born's discretion. It was expected, of course, that the eldest provide generously for those in his care. It was every man's goal to produce a male heir to continue his position in the tribe; otherwise, his goods and position went to his eldest brother. So it was that in/around 2076 BC, Abram (his original name) and Sarai (her original name), the family was childless, even though Abram was tribal leader and possessed great wealth. Sarai, knowing her husband's distress, offered up her young, pretty Egyptian handmaid, Hagar, so that Abram could produce a male heir and preserve his lineage. Sure enough, Hagar soon became pregnant, and gave birth to Ishmael… and here lies the root of the dilemma. By custom at the time, Ishmael, the Israeli-Arab cross-breed was now Abram's rightful heir. Scripture records how Hagar, once she was visibly bearing Abram's child, began acting contemptuously toward her mistress. Sarai felt something of a laughingstock within the tribe, because one of the measures of a woman's worth was her fertility. In return, Sarai began treating Hagar harshly. Sarai jealously bullied Hagar until she fled into the desert. Here, an Angel of the Lord appeared to Hagar and commanded her to return and humble herself to Sarai, which she did, on the Angel's promise that her son would become the father of a great nation.

Hagar returned and bore Abram a son, which he named Ishmael. He was a healthy boy, and flourished. Then, when Ismael was ten years old, Sarai (miraculously, at the age of 90) became pregnant and bore Abram (at 100) a son, which he named Isaac. So, what happens when there are two sons of an Israeli father…one of which was First-born, but half Arab; and the other who was late—but of pure Israeli blood? Sarai eventually demanded that Abram drive Hagar and Ishmael away, rather than see the son of an Egyptian slave sit as head of the tribe. And so, it came to be that once again, Hagar and Ishmael are banished to the desert. But God heard Ishmael's cry and promised to make of him a great nation—which he did. But under Allah, the god of Muhammad.

BUT WAIT, you may think; aren't Allah and Yehowah God one and the same with different names? Actually …*no*. Contrary to what millions have been led to believe, the two deities, as revealed in Judeo-Christian Scripture vs. the *Qur'an*, have very different sets of characteristics. As described in the Muslim Holy Book, Allah is stern, remote, forbidding, and remains above and apart from mankind. The Yehowah God of Judeo-Christianity, on the other hand, desires to reconcile with mankind and through the sacrifice of His only son Jesus Christ, spend an eternity of bliss together in Heaven. In the Muslim Paradise, however, men are rewarded for obedience to Allah by being given a bevy of female virgins who constantly regrow their virginity—*for an eternity of male carnal sexual pleasure. So, Allah's reward to a righteous Muslim man is an eternity of adolescent carnal fantasy? Does anyone else see somthing amiss here?*

Women, on the other hand, are allowed to "blissfully" serve their earthly husbands for all eternity. What's wrong with this picture? With the **Qur'an**—on Earth or in Heaven, men dominate, women serve. Now, many will be quick to point out that men *dominated* women in the Tribes of Israel as well. Yes, but Western Civilization eventually grew out of that adolescent viewpoint—but Jihadis continue to live in the medieval past…and expect everyone else to follow suit.

Strict Muslims like to claim that they force their women to cover themselves from head to toe to "honor" them. If that is so, how does it honor them to brutally slice off that same woman's clitoris for the distinct purpose of reducing her sexual pleasure? This just doesn't sound very honorable to me. And then there is the little matter of Muhammad's pedophilia; among his several wives, there was Aisha: betrothed at six years of age, and bedded at nine. Without apologies, I believe that <u>sex with a young child is just plain wrong</u>. The final evidence I will offer to prove the hypothesis that Islam degrades women as mere chattels is this: do an internet search of "greatest Muslim women", and you will come up with about TEN names, mainly from pre-medieval times. With one exception (a warrior queen in Africa centuries ago), they are mainly scholars, heiresses, and business tycoons. Contrast this with Western Civilization, which has enabled the rise of women to positions of great power and responsibility by the dozens: Cleopatra, Queen of Egypt; Boudicea, warrior-queen of the Britons; Elizabeth I of England; Catherine the Great of Russia; Marie Antoinette; Marie Curie; Eleanor Roosevelt; Golda Meier; Maggie Thatcher, Britain's "Iron Lady", etc., etc. The contrast is both stark and revealing. Throughout the Judeo-Christian world, women flourish. Under Islam, they are mere chattels under men's shadows.

Does this sound like Yehowah God? The point of all this is to underline that Muslims worship a deity which does not display the same characteristics; Allah, therefore, is NOT the same God worshipped in the West.

So, when Muhammad was writing the **Qur'an** in his cave during the early 600's, consider the historical environment in which he found himself. Ishmael's progeny was all around, but they were worshipping a pantheon of pagan idols and were generally disorganized as an ethnic group. Muhammad was, in fact, a merchant, and enjoyed wealth and prosperity. His inspirations allegedly came from visitations by the angel Gabriel. To make a long and complex story short, he morphed into a political and military leader and, with an army of 10,000 believers, he launched what was to be a rapid and diaspora-like expansion of Islam across the Middle East and Northern Africa. Resistance was met with death or enslavement, so conversions were rapid and relentless. But, at some point after his death, the interpretations of Muhammad's followers (the body of *Hadith*) acquired an aggressive and militant edge, and the Jihadists of the present-day practice some of the most brutal and uncompromising philosophies ever seen in human history. Here are just a few features of this "peaceful" belief system in practice:

— **Taqqiya:** the practice of justifying the use of deception, lying, cheating, or untruthful practices of any kind if it furthers the goals and purposes of jihadists. For instance, the "Land for Peace" deal that Yasser Arafat (PLO President) signed with Israeli Prime Minister Yitzak Rabin, brokered by US President Bill Clinton in 1993, was supposed to guarantee peace by trading land to the Palestinians in return for mutual recognition (the so-called "two-state solution"). The ink was barely dry on the treaty when the PLO began using their new land as a base for launching military operations against Israel. Under the principles of *taqqiya*, this was an entirely justified deception by Arafat, because it furthered the interests of Jihad. They simply cannot be trusted.

— **Female Genital Mutilation (FGM):** this brutal and primitive custom is deliberately intended to reduce a girl's sexual pleasure and desire, so that she is less likely to cheat on her husband. Although "officially" condemned by prominent Muslim clerics (wink, wink), this hideous practice is just one more example of how this "loving" religion views women.

— **Honor Killings:** although vehemently denied by Muslim scholars, this practice is widely practiced by many Muslims, most notably Pakistanis, as an offshoot of FGM. Case in point: a young girl of Pakistani family was gang-raped by several young Pakistani men in Great Britain. Rather than punish the perpetrators, the girl was killed by her own father to "preserve the honor of the family". *What kind of twisted mind-set could dream up such an outrageous action?* Again, this demonstrates the callous disregard of basic rights for women held by many Muslims.

— **Refusal to Assimilate:** When an immigrant enters another sovereign country by free choice, that person is normally expected to adapt and assimilate into the culture and language of the host country. America has been host to immigrants from many nations. In almost all cases, the newcomers learned the language, followed the customs, and adapted to the American way of life. They have been permitted all the blessings of our Constitution, and in return, have become part of the fabric of the nation. Not so much with Islam. In many cases, Muslim communities have deliberately isolated themselves from mainstream American culture.

— **Demands for Non-Reciprocal Accommodation:** Why do Muslims demand that Western countries change to accommodate their customs, while they are vehemently intolerant of other religions in their own countries? Muslim religious scholars give several reasons for this: (1) "Islam is a Complete System". Muslims view Islam as not just a religion, but as a complete set of rules for all aspects of life, but it doesn't go both ways. Islam takes the somewhat arrogant view that because it holds itself superior to any other viewpoint, there are no acceptable alternatives. This position is totally incompatible with American values. (2) The mandate of *Dawah*; this concept is, basically, the idea that Muslims have a duty to insist that their faith is prioritized over all foreign practices. Hence, we have Muslim-minority communities demanding that, for example, there be no pork products in school lunches (pork is forbidden to Muslims), even to non-Muslim children, because it might "offend" the Muslim children attending the same school. In some communities, Muslims belligerently block major streets for noon prayers in an "in your face" effort to compel recognition of Allah's supremacy. This, even when mosques are plentiful and nearby. In other words, the position of Muslim immigrants to Western nations is that, basically, the host nation must not only respect Muslim customs, but must be made to change their own culture and customs, as well. It is of no account, under this value system, that "the host culture was there first". Too bad, whatever Allah wants, Allah gets, even in your own back yard. Now, you understand why Western Civilization and Islamic culture and values are like oil and water: *they just don't mix!*

<><><>

Having been blessed to travel the world, live to see my 80's in good health, and deal with all manner of my fellow human beings, I am convinced of one thing: we have all been given the Breath of Life, which is God's perfect gift. I see God's greatness in everything. I do not think all of us use His gift in the ways which He intended. He gave us free will; He also allows the forces of evil to tempt us, to see what we do with those choices. Some of us attune ourselves with the chords of universal love, and some march to the harsher beat of our vices. Some of us are pulled astray in our attempt to align ourselves with the Universe, by trying to make the Universe over in the image of a god of our own fashioning. The choice is ours; God grant that we choose wisely.

In the end, we are ALL His creatures. I will close this section with a quote that embraces all of us:

"For God so loved the world that He gave His only begotten Son;
that whosoever believeth in Him should not perish, but have eternal life."
—*John 3:16*

Amen!

Did I Ever Tell You About...
THE REST OF THE STORY?

"I shall be saying this with a sigh, ages hence:
Two roads diverged in a wood, and I—
I took the one less traveled by;
and that has made all the difference."
—Robert Frost

So, I have arrived at the end of my tale, dear readers. My advisors and I agreed that *Did I Ever Tell You?* was to serve as the "handle" by which the seven books of the *Advanced Life Skills Syllabus* were to be grasped, and to encourage my audience to follow me further into that harvest of knowledge and wisdom, and so that my readers will understand how I arrived at my current position. I know now that Father God was preparing me for this, the last chapter of my life, to leave this legacy. But, for the personal events I experienced from my 30's (when Cindi and I parted ways), until the present day, suffice it to say that I led a life filled with the same challenges, highs and lows, opportunities, heartbreaks, and decisions that most everyone else has—with a few exceptions.

- I never returned to Navy Active Duty, but had a very active Reserve career for 29 years, 11 months, and 29 days. I had attained the rank of Commander (O-5), but was forced to retire by "the system" because I had failed to check the boxes necessary to attain the rank of Captain (O-6). At that time, the criteria for selection to that rank required that the member be twice selected to serve as Commanding Officer of a distinct command. I had served only once in that capacity, and because I was frequently being called up for short assignments involving my specialty areas, I was unable to play the political gamesmanship necessary to acquire one of those few, coveted command posts. My specialties included being capable in some 14 languages (including Arabic, Swahili, and Somali), and being a designated Muslim Cultural Specialist. In short, I was kept too busy to be promoted.

- For example: I was recalled to Active Duty in August of 1990 to serve on GEN Arnold Schwartzkopf's personal staff as logistics and Arabic go-to expert, supporting Operations Desert Shield, Desert Storm, and Desert Sortie; this took an entire year out of my life, but I wouldn't have traded it for the world. Naval historians documented the fact that I was *"personally responsible for establishing and maintaining the longest continuous logistical supply line in military history, extending over 8,000 nautical miles."* It was GEN Schwartzkopf who recommended me for the Bronze Star medal. We were in the middle of a relentless Scud missile bombardment from Saddam Hussein on our Command Center in Riyadh, KSA (Kingdom of Saudi Arabia). We were in the top floor of the MODA building, a fortified, 10-story structure in the heart of Riyadh. Explosions shuddered the structure about once every minute; the Iraqis were obviously targeting the building itself, hoping to score a knockout blow to our Operations Center. As the Navy's Military Sealift Command Liaison Officer to the General, I had been issued a SAT phone (Satellite Action Transmitter), a James-Bond-inspired suitcase-size device with a small dish antenna and radio-transmitter/receiver. When properly installed, it would literally allow us to make telephone calls to anywhere in the world. At the time (1990) this was state-of-the-art technology, and when I explained its capabilities to the General and his staff, he insisted that it must be installed immediately.

Since I was the only person there who had been trained in its use, the General locked eyes with me and said, "Commander, we need that gadget of yours operational, ASAP. Tell me what you need from me, and you'll have it." I told him that I needed a couple of men to help me get it up to the roof; suddenly, two Army Ranger sergeants saluted behind me. Thus, we gained access to the roof. It was pitch dark. Searchlights were scanning the skies, and anti-aircraft guns were putting streams of tracers in the skies at the incoming missile trails. The three of us quickly realized that, to add to the fun, we were in the middle of a sandstorm! I showed the Rangers how to set up the base unit, then had one of them strap the satellite dish onto my back harness. I then proceeded to climb the 40-ft radio mast that supported all of our regular communications antennae. I don't know how strong that wind was, but the mast was swaying back and forth like a reed in a storm. I moaned quietly, said a prayer to Jesus, and started climbing. A huge explosion lit up the night, and I heard a whistling *whoosh* go past my left ear.

Saddam's aim was getting better.

Several times, the wind gusted and caught the dish strapped to my back, almost pulling me off and down—waaaay down. I tried to not think about where I was: on the roof of a 10-story building, on top of a 40-ft. radio mast, in the middle of the night, in a sandstorm, with explosions and gunfire all around me. *Just breathe and go, Stevie…*I heard grandpa's soft, rumbling voice whisper through the tumult. When I finally reached the tiny steel platform at the top, the mast was swaying like a pendulum, back and forth 2-3 feet. Another explosion ripped the night, closer this time. I managed to attach the dish to the platform, aim it to where the satellite was orbiting in the sky, then calibrate the device until the welcoming "beep" confirmed that we were locked-in to the signal. Just as I started to breathe more easily, a sudden, violent gust of wind tore my grip and left me hanging by my right arm onto the cruel steel of the mast. "OH, DEAR GOD, HELP ME", I screamed. With all my strength, I pulled up and back on to the tiny platform. As I did so, I heard—and felt—a juicy RRR-IIP as the cartilage in my right rotator cuff tore apart. I swung up and onto the mast with the effort, and the jagged edges sliced through my camo jacket and tore a four-inch gash where my shoulder met my arm. I felt a warm rush of blood seeping into my uniform. To this day, I have only 50% use of my right arm. However, the SAT was successfully installed, and we hurried down to inform the General.

He noticed the blood welling through my camo tunic and called for the medics. I nodded to one of the Rangers, who handed him what looked like a regular dial telephone attached to the suitcase. "You don't even need a dime, General. Just dial "0" and tell the operator where you want to call. Compliments of the U.S. Navy, sir". I was unable to salute because two medics were bandaging up my shoulder. But the General looked me straight in the eye, and slowly saluted me. "Thank you, Commander. This is badly needed. Now go get some rest—that's an order. Dismissed!"

- Three years later: (1993) Operation Continue Hope; I was called up to Active Duty again, to organize and oversee the evacuation of some 4,000 US troops from Mogadishu, Somalia. This angry nation on the Horn of Africa was mired in constant strife by the 11 Somali clans warring with each other—and with the US—for control of the city. Mohammad Farah Aidid, chieftain of the Habr Gidin Clan, was the top dog, and it was on his orders that a cruel and barbaric genocidal conflict was being waged. Operation Continue Hope, which was designed and overseen by the United Nations, was ordered by President Bill Clinton to bring desperately needed food and medical supplies to thousands, was an utter failure. Aidid's troops seized, at gunpoint, every food truck that managed to get away from the pier. Denial of food was a weapon, by which Aidid was literally starving out the rival clans. The US, and other member nations of the UN coalition forces sent here, had finally thrown up their collective hands in despair. The lesson to be learned here is that, no matter how noble the goal, one cannot force a culture to be charitable friends if they do not wish it. Nor can "nation-building" take place within a culture which is brutally predatory to its own members. One need only to consider that piracy against passing cargo ships is one of the primary occupations of young Somalis, or consider the massive, systemic fraud being committed in Minnesota and other states. "Biting the Hand that Feeds" seems to be an accepted way of life to Somalis, due to the way that their culture has shaped generational mindsets. It is hard for Americans to grasp, but what we call "racism" in the West is actually an admirable form of "tribalism" to these Third World cultures—looking out for your own group first-- and they feel absolutely no remorse in practicing it. You can read about this entire adventure in greater detail in my "Somalia Letters" section, which is next.

- Two of my military competencies are being a Muslim Cultural Specialist, and speaking several African/Middle Eastern languages. At the end of my Navy career, I served for some years as a Technical Asset for the Special Operations Community, (i.e., Navy SEALS). The public often knows little but whisperings concerning such operations, except that some bad guy with an unpronounceable name disappears. Although often misquoted, the famous 19th century military/politician Otto von Bismarck is reputed to have said, "Men should not see their laws or their sausages being made" I can speak little of this, for obvious reasons. Suffice it to say that I learned, first-hand, that our country has the finest, most dedicated,

- and skilled warriors anywhere; and woe be unto the enemies who must learn that lesson the hard way.
- My employment with the Attorney General's Office in Cheyenne led me to become a Certified Peace Officer, and I volunteered to be a uniformed Reserve Laramie County Deputy Sheriff for seven years. I logged many hours of routine patrol, but specialized in undercover narcotics operations. Cheyenne sits at the intersection of I-25 and I-80, and is a major conduit for drugs and sex traffickers. The highlight of my short career was to serve on the Security Detail for President Ronald Reagans's visit in 1982. I got to meet him and shake his hand; he truly was one of our Nation's finest leaders. My main takeaway from my time as a law enforcement officer was an abiding respect for the men and women who serve as First Responders. They often stand as the Thin Blue Line between civil society and the forces of Evil waiting, just under the surface of things, to emerge.
- Starting with high school judo classes at the YMCA, I have studied the martial arts for most of my life, up to the present day. I hold a Shodan (first-degree black belt) in Shotokan karate, a Nidan (second-degree black belt) in Kendo—sword combat—and a Green Belt in Krav Maga. I have long been drawn to Bushido, the ancient code of the samurai warrior. It becomes a way of life that is the epitome of honor and upright action. Combined with Judeo-Christianity, it appeals to my old Boy Scout approach to life: to leave things better than I found them. I have taught martial arts for many years, having graduated over 700 students. To this day, I teach Senior Self-Defense classes to my peers as a free public service. The predators of the world respect only strength, and even the older and weaker among us cannot expect mercy from Evil, and need to be able to defend themselves. You can find my hybrid philosophy in the Advanced Life Skills Syllabus, under the title, The Ten-Fold Path. In the intervening years between then and now, my life mirrored what pretty much any middle-aged man goes through. I had a series of relationships, continued my studies, and started recording the material that you are reading today.

I ultimately achieved a lifetime goal of earning my PhD in Religious Studies, with a focus on Ancient Languages (Greek, Latin, Phoenician, Aramaic, etc.). The rest of this effort is my Advanced Life Skills Syllabus, a series of seven mini-books addressing the spectrum of human knowledge, applied in daily life. But first, *The Somalia Letters*, and *Roadbirds I Have Known*, two booklets which, I hope, will both inform and entertain…

<><><>
"The moving finger writes;
And, having writ, moves on.
Not all thy piety nor wit
Shall lure it back to cancel half a line,
Nor all your tears wash out a word of it."

—Omar Khayyam, 1122 AD

BONUS

SOMALIA LETTERS

Author's Note: The Somalia Letters were written under combat conditions in and around Mogadishu, Somalia, between January and March, 1994. It was captured using a primitive, military-issue field computer/printer with limited font selections. In the interests of preserving the authenticity of a piece written (literally) to the sounds of sporadic gunfire, I have left it unedited and in its original format.

—S.M.

Somalia Letters ...
I Have Arrived?

01 Feb 1994

I ARRIVED IN MOGADISHU EARLY SATURDAY 22 JAN, NONE THE WORSE FOR WEAR AFTER A 5-DAY ODYSSEY THROUGH GREENSBORO, CHARLOTTE, GREAT BRITAIN, GERMANY, AND EGYPT. I HAD OF COURSE SEEN THE SAME MEDIA COVERAGE YOU HAVE, READ BOOKS AND BEEN BRIEFED BY FOLKS WHO HAVE BEEN HERE BEFORE, BUT NOTHING QUITE PREPARES YOU FOR THE REALITY OF THIS PLACE. MOGADISHU (THE NAME MAKES ME THINK OF A MESSY SNEEZE) DEFINES THE TERM "THIRD WORLD". THE HEAT, DUST, SMELL, BABEL OF NOISES HUMAN AND MECHANICAL, THE ATMOSPHERE OF NOT-SO-QUIET DESPERATION, ALL ASSAULT THE SENSES AT ONCE. SAND, AS FINE AS POWDER AND THE COLOR OF BONE ASH, FILLS THE AIR SO THAT THE COLORS OF OBJECTS ARE NOT TRUE TO THEIR POSITIONS IN THE SPECTRUM. LAND, SKY, PLANTS,

ANIMALS, STRUCTURES--AND PEOPLE--ARE ALL JUST DIFFERENT SHADES OF BONE ASH. ON PEOPLE, THOUGH, IT BECOMES A SORT OF PALE GREY SLUDGE THAT CAKES IN LITTLE PATCHES AND STREAKS ON FACES AND ARMS. THE SOMALIS THEMSELVES REFER TO ONE PART OF THEIR COUNTRY AS "GUBAN" OR "BURNED LAND".

MOGADISHU, I AM TOLD, IS BY COMPARISON LUSH AND FERTILE; GUBAN MUST BE THE BACKSIDE OF HELL.

THE MISSION IS NOW CALLED "OPERATION CONTINUE HOPE". WHAT STARTED OUT AS A WELL-INTENTIONED EFFORT TO RESCUE INNOCENTS FROM STARVATION HAS US, AND THE OTHER UN NATIONS, BACKING TOWARD THE DOOR WITH GUNS DRAWN. THE POLITICIANS CAN PUT ANY SPIN ON IT THEY LIKE; THE BOTTOM LINE IS THAT THE FAMILY OF NATIONS HAS THROWN UP ITS HANDS AND IS LEAVING THIS CANTANKEROUS ORPHAN TO ITS FATE. THERE IS A MESSAGE HERE AS TIMELESS AS IT IS FREQUENTLY IGNORED: THAT NO ONE CAN FORCE ANY PEOPLE TO BE CHARITABLE ASSOCIATES IF THEY DO NOT WISH IT. IN THE END, THERE MUST BE VICTORS AND VANQUISHED, SUPERIOR AND SUBORDINATE, JUST AS IT HAS BEEN SINCE MANKIND FIRST SWUNG A CLUB. ANYONE WHO THINKS OTHERWISE HAS BEEN READING TOO MANY FAIRY TALES, AND NEEDS TO SPEND SOME TIME HERE OR IN BOSNIA TO COMPLETE THEIR EDUCATION.

I HAVE BEEN HERE A LITTLE OVER A WEEK AND MY DAI-

LY ROUTINE IS SET. SURROUNDED BY BATTALIONS OF ARMY/AIR FORCE TYPES, I'VE ESTABLISHED A LITTLE CORNER THAT SAYS "US NAVY", WITH THE. CHARTS AND EQUIPMENT THAT ARE TOOLS OF MY TRADE — SEALIFT. "WHAT ARE YOU DOING HERE?" IS THE SOMEWHAT CHALLENGING QUESTION I OFTEN GET FROM STRANGERS. "I'M HERE TO GET YOU HOME", I REPLY, AND INSTANTLY A CUP OF COFFEE IS THRUST INTO MY HAND, WIDE SMILES CREASE THE SUNBURNED, DUSTY FACES, AND I AM ONE OF THE FAMILY. UNLIKE DURING THE GULF WAR, WHICH HAD AN AIR OF FLAG-DRAPED DERRING-DO ABOUT IT, EVERYONE INVOLVED IN OPERATION "CONTINUE HOPE" HAS ONLY ONE--TO LEAVE AS QUICKLY AS POSSIBLE.

MY ROUTINE IS TO RISE AT 0500 (THIS IS GUARANTEED BY THE SPECIAL FORCES PLATOON BEHIND MY HOOCH, CRANKING UP THEIR VEHICLES FOR MORNING PATROL), GET IN MY DAILY WORKOUT, SHOWER, DRESS, EAT, AND BE AT MY OFFICE BY 0700. THIS IS NOT A DIFFICULT COMMUTE BECAUSE THE REDEPLOYMENT COORDINATION CENTER (RCC) WHERE I WORK IS ONLY ACROSS 100 YDS OF SAND FROM WHERE I SLEEP. WE ARE VIRTUALLY ON THE EQUATOR AND TEMPS ARE 90'S, BUT SURPRISINGLY COOL/BREEZY AT NIGHT.

MY DAY IS FILLED WITH REPORTS, PHONE CALLS, TRACKING SHIP MOVEMENTS, ATTENDING BRIEFINGS, AND THE MYRIAD OTHER TASKS INVOLVED IN MOVING 5,000 PEOPLE AND 1,000 VEHICLES OUT OF HERE BY 31 MARCH. THERE IS

NO REL "LUNCH", YOU GRAB AN MRE (MEAL-READY-TO-EAT, MUMMIFIED RATIONS NUKED AND SEALED YEARS AGO) AND KEEP WORKING. THE PACE WINDS DOWN BY 1800 OR SO, AND HOT DINNERS ARE SERVED AT THE MESS TENT. THE FOOD IS EXCELLENT AND I EAT LIKE A HORSE, BUT I AM LOSING WEIGHT ANYWAY DUE TO. ACTIVITY LEVEL. THE WORST PART ABOUT MEALS IS FIGHTING OFF THE HORDES OF FLIES THAT WANT TO SHARE. WE HAVE ALL LEARNED TO EAT VERY QUICKLY FOR THIS REASON. THERE IS NO ESCAPE, ANYWHERE, FROM THE BUGS OR THE DUST. EVEN THE GENERALS MUST SWAT, CUSS, AND SWALLOW SILICON WITH THEIR STEAKS LIKE THE LOWLIEST PRIVATE OR NAVY COMMANDER.

MY OFFICE IN AN AIR-CONDITIONED TEMPORARY STRUCTURE, AND THAT IS A BLESSING, BUT QUARTERS ARE A 9X9 TRAILER CUBICLE WITH ONE TINY WINDOW, A COT, AND A FAN. TEMP INSIDE AT THE END OF THE DAY IS 110-115 DEGREES. THANK GOD FOR THE FAN, BUT THEN HOPE THE POWER DOESN'T GO OUT, WHICH IT DOES FREQUENTLY. WHEN THAT HAPPENS, EVERYONE SITS OUTSIDE IN THE DARK BREEZE UNTIL IT COMES BACK ON. SLEEPING OUTSIDE IS DANGEROUS DUE TO POISONOUS SNAKES, SCORPIONS, SPIDERS, CENTIPEDES, AND A HOST OF OTHER CREEPY-CRAWLIES THAT WANT TO CUDDLE UP. TENT DWELLERS USE NETTING AND GALLONS OF INSECTICIDE, STILL GET BITTEN OCCASIONALLY SO I CONSIDER MYSELF FORTUNATE TO HAVE A WOODEN FLOOR AND

ONLY FLIES/MOSQUITOES/HEAT TO DEAL WITH. NEEDLESS TO SAY, I SPEND A LOT MORE TIME IN MY OFFICE THAN NECESSARY TO FINISH MY WORK.

THERE IS A SURPRISING NUMBER OF FEMALE MILITARY MEMBERS HERE, ALL OF WHOM CARRY GUNS, GRUNT, AND SUFFER ALONG WITH THE MEN....WHINING GETS NO SYMPATHY FROM ANY QUARTER, ANYWAY. I AM IMPRESSED WITH THEIR TOUGHNESS AND HAVE LOST ANY VESTIGE OF GENDER BIAS I MAY HAVE STILL RETAINED (YES, REALLY!) FROM LESS POLITICALLY CORRECT TIMES.

IF WE NEEDED ANY REMINDERS THAT OUR WELCOME HERE IS UP, THE CLOSE AND SPORADIC GUNFIRE OUTSIDE THE PERIMETER SERVES THAT PURPOSE. WE ALL GO ARMED EVERYWHERE, EVEN TO THE HEAD. UNAUTHORIZED SOMALIS SNEAK THROUGH THE PERIMETER OR ARE ALLOWED THROUGH BY OUR UN EGYPTIAN ALLIES WHO ARE RUNNING A BRISK BLACK MARKET OPERATION IN STOLEN U.S. GOV'T PROPERTY. THE ARMY SPECIAL FORCES GUYS ADVISED ME TO SLEEP WITH

MY 9MM UNDER THE PILLOW, UNHOLSTERED. I AM GLAD THEY ARE NEXT DOOR. THE GOOD LORD WILLING AND THE CREEK DON'T RISE, WE WILL ALL BE OUT OF HERE BY EARLY MARCH. I CAN DEAL WITH ANYTHING FOR THAT LONG, ESPECIALLY WHEN I CONSIDER THE HARDSHIPS EXPERIENCED BY THOSE ALREADY HERE FOR MONTHS. LIFE WILL GET EVEN

BETTER NEXT FRIDAY WHEN MY MARISAT UNIT ARRIVES FROM JAPAN AND I CAN MAKE (VERY LIMITED) TELEPHONE CALLS.

I WOULD LOVE TO HEAR FROM ANYONE BACK HOME. IT'S LONELY OUT HERE. PLEASE WRITE TO:

CDR STEVE MCMIKLE, USNR us FORCES SOMALIA/Rec
UNIT 0659, CMR #11
APO AE 09863-0659

HAVING A WONDERFUL TIME
BUT BE GLAD YOU'RE NOT HERE!

Loading the Troops

Somalia Letters ...
Two Whole Weeks?

07 Feb 1994

Working on my tan

DEAR FRIENDS:

I AM NOW A VETERAN OF TWO WHOLE WEEKS IN-COUNTRY SOMALIA, BUT IT FEELS LIKE TWO MONTHS. THE DAYS BLUR TOGETHER IN A MERCIFUL RUSH THAT LEAVES LITTLE TIME TO THINK ABOUT HARDSHIPS AND DANGERS. THEY HAVE GIVEN ME AN END DATE: MARCH 15 (THE "IDES OF MARCH"). FROM HERE I WILL GO TO LONDON AND WASHINGTON FOR DEBRIEFS BEFORE HEADING HOME AT LAST...BUT THIRTY-EIGHT MORE TICK MARKS ON THE WALL.

ONE OF THE MOST UNIQUE THINGS ABOUT THIS MISSION IS THE TRULY INTER NATIONAL FLAVOR OF IT. BESIDES DAILY OPPORTUNITIES TO PRACTICE MY ARABIC, GERMAN, AND GREEK, THERE IS A VERITABLE BANQUET OF DIFFERENT PEOPLES TO INTERACT WITH: ROMANIANS, RUSSIANS, PAKI-

STANIS, INDIANS, BANGLADESHIS, KOREANS, TURKS, ITALIANS, KENYANS, UGANDANS, AUSSIES, NORWEGIANS--AND THOSE ARE JUST THE ONES LIVING AND WORKING IN MY IMMEDIATE VICINITY. PIDGIN ENGLISH AND FRENCH ARE THE ONLY LANGUAGES MOST OF US HAVE IN COMMON; GESTURES AND SMILES ARE UNIVERSAL. THE INDIANS AND PAKISTANIS ARE TECHNICALLY AT WAR IN THEIR HOMELANDS, BUT DECLARE A TRUCE WHILE HERE. THE RUSSIANS OPERATE THE EMBASSY-AIRPORT HELICOPTER SHUTTLE, AND I MARVEL EACH TIME AT FLYING IN A RUSSIAN CHOPPER WITH SMILING CREWMEN WHO WERE OUR COLD-WAR FOES 4 YEARS AGO.

 I MUST DRIVE FROM THE AIRPORT COMPOUND TO THE PORT DAILY, THROUGH A HALF-MILE STRIP OF NO-MAN'S-LAND WHERE THE HOSTILE FORCES OF GENERAL MOHAMMED AIDID, HE OF THE NINE LIVES, HOLD SWAY JUST THE OTHER SIDE OF THE RAZOR WIRE. TWO BRADLEY FIGHTING VEHICLES HAVE THEIR GUNS TRAINED INTO THE STRIP AS I PASS IN MY JEEP, TO DISCOURAGE SNIPERS. NIGHT PASSAGES ARE THE MOST DANGEROUS, AND I HAVE ONLY HAD TO MAKE ONE OF THOSE SO FAR. DURING THE DAY RUNS, WOMEN AND CHILDREN PRESS AGAINST THE CRUEL WIRE TO STRETCH OUT HANDS, BEGGING FOR FOOD OR BOTTLED WATER. THE TYPICAL SOMALI WOMAN IN THIS PART OF THE COUNTRY BEARS AN AVERAGE OF TEN CHILDREN, ONLY

THREE OF WHOM WILL SURVIVE TO ADOLESCENCE. THE REAL SHAME IS, THIS IS PRIMARILY DUE TO CLAN WARFARE AND RESULTING USE OF FOOD AND MEDICAL CARE, OR THE DENIAL OF THEM, AS WEAPONS. THE FACES OF THESE PEOPLE REFLECT NOT JUST NEED, BUT BITTERNESS AS WELL, AND THEY ARE EQUALLY READY TO HURL ROCKS OR PLEAS FOR A HANDOUT. THESE SOMALIS ARE NOT HAPPY WE ARE LEAVING, BECAUSE WE REPRESENT A SOURCE OF WEALTH. THEY ALSO KNOW THAT WHEN WE LEAVE

THE KILLING WILL RESUME. THE DICHOTOMY IS THAT THEY ARE ANGRY WE ARE LEAVING, AND ANGRY THAT WE ARE STILL HERE. IT IS LIKE AN INFANT'S MINDLESS AND TERRIBLE RAGE AGAINST THINGS IT DOES NOT UNDERSTAND AND CANNOT CONTROL, AND JUST AS FRUSTRATING TO DEAL WITH. FOR THE SOMALIS, GOD HELP THEM, ANOTHER HOLOCAUST AWAITS ONLY OUR DEPARTURE.

THE UN IS RELYING, OFFICIALLY, ON A SO-CALLED "SOMALI POLICE FORCE" TO MAINTAIN ORDER AND FORM THE MATRIX FOR AN EMBRYONIC GOVERNMENT. WE ARE BUSILY SUPPLYING THEM WITH SURPLUS TANKS AND OTHER FAIRLY SOPHISTICATED WEAPONRY, HOPING TO ESTABLISH THEM AS A CREDIBLE FORCE TO WHICH THE UN CAN PASS THE BATON. THE FLAW IN THIS STRATEGY IS

CLEAR TO THE LOWLIEST ARMY PRIVATE (BUT NOT, SO IT SEEMS, TO THOSE IN HIGHER OFFICE): THE CHIEF OF THE

NEWLY-CREATED POLICE FORCE IS NONE OTHER THAN GEN AHMED JILAO ADDO, WHOSE REPUTATION FOR MURDER AND TORTURE OF INNOCENTS IS SECOND TO NONE. HE IS NOT THE WORST OF THE BAD GUYS, BUT HIS DEEDS AND MOTIVES ARE FAR FROM PURE. JILAO IS THE SWORN-BLOOD ENEMY OF FARAH AIDID, WHO HOLDS MOST OF MOGADISHU, WHERE THE POLICE. FORCE IS BASED. WHAT'S WRONG WITH THIS PICTURE? ALL WE HAVE DONE, IN THE END, IS FORCE-FEED SOMALIA WHILE WE GIVE HER CRUEL AND DESPOTIC LITTLE CAESARS MORE EFFICIENT MEANS OF KILLING ONE ANOTHER. I AM TOO DEPRESSED BY THIS SUBJECT TO WRITE ANY MORE ABOUT IT. THE FACES OF THOSE CHILDREN, CRYING BEHIND THE DUSTY COILS OF RAZOR WIRE AND SURROUNDED BY THE STENCH OF DEATH AND DECAY, WILL REMAIN WITH ME LONG AFTER I'VE SHAKEN SOMALIA'S VENOMOUS DUST FROM MY FEET.

LAST NIGHT, ABOUT 2300, A FIREFIGHT ERUPTED OUTSIDE THE PERIMETER, AND THE SOUNDS OF EXPLOSIONS AND GUNFIRE HAD US ALL ROLLING OUT AND SCRAMBLING FOR CLOTHING AND WEAPONS IN THE DARK. A FEW STRAY ROUNDS FELL INSIDE THE PERIMETER, BUT WE SUSTAINED NO CASUALTIES (MY SKINNED KNEES AND ELBOWS DIDN'T COUNT). AIDID IS STILL IN CONTROL OF THE CITY AND HE LIKES TO GENTLY REMIND US OF THAT FACT FROM TIME TO TIME. THE POLITICIANS ARE PRAYING THAT HE WILL LET US

BACK AWAY, SWEATING AND GRINNING AT THE SAME TIME, WITHOUT PROVOKING THE U.S. INTO A MAJOR RETALIATORY ACTION THAT MIGHT DELAY THE WITHDRAWAL DATE. THE JOKER IS THAT FARAH AIDID WILL GAIN FACE WITH THE SOMALIS BY APPEARING TO KICK US OUT, SO HE'LL PROBABLY GET FEISTIER AS MARCH 31 NEARS.

ON A LIGHTER NOTE, IT SEEMS I MUST MAKE AN OFFICIAL TRIP TO MOMBASA (KENYA) AROUND 15 FEB. AFTER MY WORK THERE IS FINISHED, I HOPE TO TAKE A 2-DAY PHOTO-SAFARI, SOMETHING I HAVE WANTED TO DO FOR YEARS. THERE IS SOME GOODNESS TO BE FOUND IN ALL THINGS. MOMBASA, I AM TOLD, HAS A WORLD-CLASS BRITISH PUB WITH COLD PINTS OF KINGFISHER BITTERS. IT WOULD BE A SHAME TO LEAVE THIS EXOTIC PLACE WITHOUT EXPLORING ITS WONDERS, BOTH NATURAL AND MAN-MADE.

MY MARISAT IS STUCK IN DIEGO GARCIA, SO I HAVE BEEN UNABLE TO TELEPHONE OUT. I HOPE TO GET IT PUT ON THE WEEKLY BIRD THIS DIRECTION SOON, BUT GETTING ANYTHING DONE OUT HERE IS LIKE HERDING CHICKENS. MEANWHILE, I AM STILL ALIVE AND KICKING, AND WORKING ON MY SUNTAN.

WISHING ALL THE BEST FOR YOU AND YOURS AS 1994 UNFOLDS, AND AS THE SOMALIS SAY, "NAHBAD GELYO!" (STAY COOL)...

Somalia Letters ...
ISKA WARAN!

21 Feb 1994

Herding the cats.

THAT IS ONE OF THE FEW POLITE PHRASES (A GREETING) USED HERE IN THE LAST UNSPOILED PARADISE OF SOMALIA. LESS ENDEARING BUT CONSIDERABLY MORE COMMON IS "BEERKA IYO MADAXA DHULKA DHIG, HA DHAQAAQIN!" (LIE FACE DOWN AND DON'T MOVE OR I'LL BLOW YOU AWAY). BERLITZ WOULD WEEP. UNFORTUNATELY, THERE ARE NO REAL "CULTURAL OPPORTUNITIES" TO LEARN ABOUT THESE PEOPLE. WE ARE MERELY PALLBEARERS AT THE FUNERAL, AND THE CUSTOMER IS, QUITE INCIDENTALLY, STILL ALIVE. PERHAPS THE MAYANS & EASTER ISLANDERS BECAME EXTINCT THIS WAY, TOO: SPIRITUAL GANGRENE.

I AM COLLECTING MANY PHOTOGRAPHS OF THIS EXPERIENCE, SOME WITH A CAMERA BUT MORE WITH VIVID IMAGES BURNED INTO THE FILM OF MEMORY. OF THESE, MANY ARE PAINFUL, BUT OTHERS ARE THOUGHT-PROVOKING, PROFOUND, DROLL, LUDICROUS, BITTER-SWEET, AND EVEN OUT-

RAGEOUSLY FUNNY. HERE ARE A FEW TEASERS FROM MY COLLECTION, DESTINED PERHAPS TO BE THE NEXT "MASH"...

THROUGH THE DARKEST COMMUNAL SHOWER WITH GUN AND CAMERA

SOMETHING WONDROUS HAPPENS TO GROUPS OF MEN WHO FIND THEMSELVES ABRUPTLY NAKED IN THE SAME ROOM, ESPECIALLY WHEN ALL ARE STRANGERS. NERVOUS, FORCED LAUGHTER ECHOES LIKE THE SOUND OF DOGS COUGHING. THE MEN GRUNT AND SCRATCH THEIR BODY HAIR. VOICES DEEPEN, AND EVERYONE ASSUMES A SORT OF ROLLING SWAGGER, LIKE GLADIATORS COMING IN FROM A TOUGH DAY AT THE COLISEUM. THE UNSPOKEN RULE IN THE COMMUNAL SHOWER IS: NEVER, BUT NEVER, BEND OVER TO PICK UP DROPPED SOAP. A MAN WHO ACCIDENTALLY DROPS HIS SOAP WILL INSTANTLY FREEZE, AND JUST LIKE IN THE E.F. HUTTON COMMERCIAL, ALL CONVERSATION CEASES AT ONCE. MOISTURE THAT IS NOT FROM THE SHOWER APPEARS ON HIS BROW, AND ALL THE OTHER MEN WATCH OUT OF THE CORNERS OF THEIR EYES AS THE HAPLESS WARRIOR EXECUTES A GRACEFUL, COURTSEY-LIKE DIP TO RETRIEVE THE ERRANT BAR, CAREFULLY TURNING TO FACE HIS COMRADES AS HE DOES SO. ACCOMPANIED BY THIS MOVEMENT, AS SMOOTHLY AND SIMULTANEOUSLY AS THE SHIFTING OF A SCHOOL OF FISH, THE OTHER MEN WILL MAKE A HALF-TURN

TO THE SIDE AWAY FROM THE SUBJECT. THIS MANEUVER MUST BE ACCOMPANIED BY MORE GROWLS, GRUNTS, AND PROFANITIES IN BASSO PROFUNDO BY EVERYONE PRESENT, BUT ESPECIALLY BY THE SUBJECT, WHO IS OBLIGED TO GROWL LOUDEST OF ALL.

BY THE ELABORATE SOCIAL RULES OF THE MALE COMMUNAL SHOWER, THE MAN WHO DROPS HIS SOAP TOO OFTEN IS AN UNHAPPY PARIAH WITH WHOM NO OTHER MAN WILL GRUNT OR SCRATCH. I HAVE OFTEN WONDERED IF MILITARY WOMEN HAVE CORRESPONDING RITUALS, LIKE HUMMING DORIS DAY TUNES OR SOME-SUCH. STILL, MY PURSUIT OF THIS MYSTERY IS OF COURSE LIMITED BY BARRIERS WHICH I WILL NOT COMPROMISE, EVEN IN THE NAME OF PURE SCIENTIFIC RESEARCH.

MONKEY BUSINESS

"WHAT?", I SAID AGAIN, NOT BELIEVING WHAT I HAD HEARD THE FIRST TIME. "YOU NEED A DIPLOMATIC CLEARANCE FOR A MONKEY?"

THE ARMY CORPORAL WAS SHIFTING NERVOUSLY FROM ONE FOOT TO ANOTHER IN FRONT OF MY DESK. "HE'S NOT A MONKEY, SIR, HE'S A BUSHBABY—AN ENDANGERED SPECIES--AND WE'VE ALREADY GOT A SPONSOR FOR HIM IN THE STATES". THIS UNLIKELY CONVERSATION STARTED ME ON A BIZARRE THREE-DAY PROJECT WHICH COULD ONLY HAPPEN

HERE IN LA-LA LAND. SEEMS THIS BUSHBABY OR WHATEVER JUST CLIMBED UP IN THE SOLDIER'S LAP WHILE HE WAS SITTING IN A JEEP, AND

 THE NEW SURROGATE PARENT WAS DETERMINED TO SAVE THIS ONE REFUGEE FROM THE CHAOS OF SOMALIA. BUSHBABIES ARE NOT INDIGENOUS TO THIS PART OF AFRICA. HOW THIS ONE GOT HERE, ALLAH KNOWS, BUT HIS DESTINY AS AN EXOTIC ENTREE FOR SOME LOCAL WAS CERTAIN UNLESS HE WAS SMUGGLED OUT. THE COMPLICATIONS OF DOING THAT ARE ENORMOUS. I CAN TELL YOU THAT IT WOULD LIKELY BE EASIER TO GET SADDAM HUSSEIN A VISIT TO DISNEY WORLD THAN WHAT WE WENT THROUGH TO GET THAT BUSHBABY TO THE STATES. MESSAGE TRAFFIC FLEW AROUND THE WORLD & BACK, BUREAUCRATS FORCED WAYS THROUGH ORDINARILY IMPASSABLE BARRIERS, WHILE A FAMOUS ENVIRONMENTAL GROUP HOVERED SOLICITOUSLY OVER EVERY STEP AND MEMORANDUM UNTIL THE ANSWER WAS YES. AT LAST, WITH FANFARE BEFITTING THE OFFSPRING OF ROYALTY, THE BUSHBABY FLEW FIRST-CLASS WITH HIS ARMY SPONSOR TO HIS NEW HOME IN AN AMERICAN UNIVERSITY-RUN ANIMAL SANCTUARY, WHERE PEACE AND BOUNTY ALL HIS PRECIOUS LIFE WERE ASSURED BY AN ADORING PUBLIC.....

 +++

 HAVING SEEN THE LITTLE RASCAL SAFELY OFF, I STARTed past the razor wire surrounding the airstrip, back to my hooch. An aged Somali man sat in the dust outside the wire with downcast eyes. His left foot had been injured, and was swollen up like a grotesque purple sausage. Flies swarmed around the suppurating wound; he did not try to wave them off as they buzzed and bored into his mangled flesh. The old man looked up at me without expression, proud even in his obvious misery. "Qoloma ayaad reerkaagu?" I asked, "Where is your family?"

He spread his hands and grinned toothless in a gesture of resignation, but caught my tossed water-bottle deftly, nodding his thanks. "Hub ma sigarra?" he asked, then it was my turn to spread my hands to show I had no cigarettes to give him. Too bad, I thought, perhaps he should have asked for a diplomatic clearance. But then again, human beings, even the old and the sick, are not considered endangered species...

THE JERSEY LILLY

The strikingly beautiful girl, suddenly next to me at the bar in the Mombasa Beach Hotel, could be a fashion model for Victoria's Secret. In Mombasa on a precious, 48-hour parole from Mogadishu, I am

STILL GIDDY FROM MY FIRST BEER IN OVER A MONTH. THE GIRL'S SMILE SWIMS LIKE A MIRAGE BEFORE MY EYES. SHE HAS A YOUNG, COOKIES-AND-MILK-NEXT-DOOR LOOK, BUT IS OBVIOUSLY VERY MUCH A WOMAN. HER FIGURE, FORMED FROM THE STUFF OF SAILORS' DREAMS, LITERALLY THRUSTS ITSELF AT ME FROM A DISTANCE OF ONLY THREE HEART STOPPING FEET, THROUGH A CLINGY BLOUSE THAT IS HAVING A TOUGH TIME CONTAINING ITS CARGO. I FEEL MY PALMS START TO SWEAT. I SWIVEL AROUND IN THE RECONNOITERING MANNER ONE INSTINCTIVELY ADOPTS IN AFRICA. NO ONE ELSE AROUND. UH-OH....

"SO WHAT ARE YOU DOING IN MOMBASA?", SHE ASKS. A LONG SWALLOW OF BEER BEFORE I EXPLAIN THE MOGADISHU MISSION IN GENERAL TERMS, AND

MY BRIEF RESPITE OF SANITY IN KENYA BEFORE HEADING BACK IN TWO DAYS.

"HOW ABOUT YOU?" I ASK. HER RESPONSE IS PUNCTUATED BY A LANGUOROUSLY WET SMILE AND AN ARCHED EYEBROW.

"WHY, I'M WORKING HERE FOR THE SUMMER, TO PAY FOR COLLEGE TUITION. I'M FROM JERSEY, NAME'S TANYA, WHAT'S YOURS?". I SHAKE THE OFFERED HAND, CAREFULLY MANICURED AND SURPRISINGLY COOL TO THE TOUCH. VERY GRATEFUL FOR ANY CIVIL TOPIC OF CONVERSATION, I INTRODUCE MYSELF AND ASK, "WHAT SCHOOL DO YOU ATTEND?"

"HAVEN'T DECIDED YET. BUT I KNOW THEY ALL COST BUCKS. I CAN'T STUDY AND WORK AT THE SAME TIME, SO I'M WORKING THIS SEMESTER".

"WHOM ARE YOU WORKING FOR?"

AGAIN THE WET SMILE. "WHOEVER HIRES ME. I'M A TOUR GUIDE".

NOW, OTHER GUYS MAY HAVE GOTTEN IT BY NOW, BUT I SUPPOSE THAT I'VE ACCUMULATED TOO MUCH SAND BETWEEN MY EARS IN SOMALIA SO I ASK, QUITE STUPIDLY,

"OH, SO YOU MUST HAVE SPENT A LOT OF TIME IN MOMBASA".

"NEVER SET EYES ON THE PLACE BEFORE LAST MONTH."

OH. NOW I GET IT. WHAT'S MORE, SHE SEES THAT I GET IT. THE "TOUR GUIDE", LIKE THE VELDT LIONESS SHE IS, MOVES IN FOR THE KILL. "CARE FOR A TOUR? YOU CAN BUY ME A DRINK FIRST, AND WE'LL TALK ABOUT WHICH AREAS YOU'RE MOST INTERESTED IN". THIS REMARK IS ACCOMPANIED BY A SLIGHT SHIFTING OF THE CLINGY BLOUSE IN MY DIRECTION, LIKE TWIN M1 TANK BARRELS TAKING AIM. MY MOUTH INSTANTLY BECOMES BONE-DRY, AND MY FACE FEELS HOT AS A BLAST FURNACE. I'M BLUSHING, FOR GOD'S SAKE!

+++

MERCIFULLY, THE JERSEY LILLY SENSES THAT I AM NOT THE PREY SHE SEEKS, AND GOES TO POWDER HER PREDATORY NOSE. I ESCAPE OUTSIDE TO THE BRIGHT SUNSHINE, TO A

STREET FILLED WITH THROBBING AFRICAN RHYTHMS AND THE MULTI-COLORED STALLS OF VENDORS. THEY, TOO, ARE INTERESTED IN THE CONTENTS OF MY WALLET, BUT IN THEIR CASE THE PROCESS OF EXTRACTION IS FAR LESS TRAUMATIC, AND THE RESULTS (ULTIMATELY) FAR MORE ENJOYABLE.

Pentagon Officials

Tying Her Up to the Pier

Old Russian MIG

Somalia Letters …
"Tales From the Scrypt"

25 Feb 1994

JAMBO, Friends!

Welcome to yet another episode of "Tales From the Scrypt". Now, coming to you live from the captivating ambiance of the Mogadishu Hilton's Sky Room (so named because the roof was blown off by mortar fire), is our intrepid reporter with this week's selection.

Night sounds

One of the diversions available here is studying the various sounds in and around the compound at night. They range from the exotic to the mundane, but each tells a story, amplified in the mind's eye.

Join us now as we enter the-mysterious-great-African Darkside ....

+++

— **"wheeeeeeEEET"**: a mosquito making final approach and alighting on target. The *Aedes aegypti,* not the national bird of Somalia, has a proboscis the size of a soda straw and enjoys insect repellent as a condiment. Your choice of diseases available courtesy of this visitor includes Dengue fever, cramps, Chikungunya fever, Crimean-Congo Hemorrhagic fever, and O'nyong-nyong, which sounds suspiciously like the daily special at an Irish-Chinese restaurant. You only live twice.

+++

— **"skitter, skitter, skitter"**: a large scorpion crawling across your plywood floor. One's first impulse is to leap up and smash him, but that action is unwise until you get a better idea of his location. The sting from one of these babies, while not fatal, will swell you up like a balloon and put you down for several days. Defense: Shine your flashlight on the floor, reach for your boots and shake them out (he could be inside). Put on your boots and turn on the overhead lights. If you fail to find the critter, it is tough to get back to sleep, wondering where he's holed up. Scorpions are nocturnal, like vampires. I found one sleeping, my toothbrush in his fierce embrace, in my shaving kit. His final reveille was not a pleasant event for either one of us.

+++

— **"chewy-chewy-chewy-chewy"**: the constant helicopter gunship patrols overhead. This is a background noise to everything else, but is quite comforting because the threat of instant retaliation, using the night vision equipment the hueys shoot through, keeps the bad guys' heads down. The pilots of the "Little Birds" are the unsung heroes of this operation, as they expose themselves to gunfire for our protection on the ground. We sleep better at the sound of their passage.

+++

— **"chun-ga, chun-ga, CHUNK-ga-ga-ga"**: the dreaded sound of the camp generator going down for the umpty-seventh time. When this happens, the darkness is complete, save for flashlights, and the fans that keep the air moving in the hooches stop. Everyone gets up when the generator quits, as much out of discomfort as because it could be sabotage and the prelude to a sneak attack. So far, it has always been an equipment malfunction or a breaker going out, and we take turns holding our flashlights for the technicians as they fix the trouble.

One of these events turned unexpectedly fun when someone brought a bag of marshmallows, and we had an impromptu roast over a scrap lumber campfire—reminding me of college sing-alongs, long ago and far away, until Security noted that we made great illuminated sniper targets.

+++

— **"spat, spat":** incoming small-arms fire, hitting the sandbags around the hooches. Enough of these would sound like big raindrops, and I have always loved the sound of rain at night, but this one gives no such pleasant feeling. Au contraire, ma cherie.

+++

— **"dum-dum, dum-dum":** the A.K-4,'J assault rifle, favored weapon of the enemy. Clint Eastwood was right, it makes a distinctive sound when fired in your direction. Sometimes followed closely by "spat, spat". I do not know what our M-16s sound like to them, but I'm told it is a sharper, high-pitched sound which more often precedes, for the luckless target, complete and eternal silence—jolly good show.

+++

— **"chROWMMED":** incoming mortar fire, or sometimes a bomb or mine detonation. These are usually distant but occasionally close enough to rattle the window screen. The one to fear is the one you DON'T hear, so they say, but how do "they" know? When I was a Boy Scout & the scoutmaster pointed out poisonous mushrooms, I always thought of the poor guy who unwittingly demonstrated which was which.

+++

— **"skrik, skrik, skrik, skrik"**: the cheerful, cricket-like rhythm of a regulation nylon and aluminum Army cot being actively occupied by two soldiers at once. As I have said, there are some 300 female military personnel among us, & shyness is a regressive characteristic which has been, so to speak, bred out of many of them. The unwritten but religiously adhered-to Code of the Compound dictates that all uninvolved parties studiously ignore this Night Sound, even when it occurs in the immediate proximity, out of a mixture of respect, reverence, and envy. Skrikking occurs in cyclic series of widely varying intensity and duration, usually terminating with a single pronounced "SK-RAAAAAWK". Listening carefully, one can then hear a huge collective sigh of relief from the audience, who is free to attempt to get back to sleep. On at least one occasion, however, a skrikking started normally enough but soon took on a strange and discordant note, followed quickly by a sharp "SMACK!" that rangout in the night, then complete silence. None of us slept well.

Rap on, Opus

Billy is a lively African-American kid from New Orleans, who joined the Army to escape the fate of so many other young black men raised in the bowels of big cities. He has an infectious smile almost as wide as his ears and performs his duty as mess cook with energy and skill.

Billy is my next-door cell-mate in the crowded hooch where

we sleep, has a bodacious boom-box with rap music collection to match, and therein lies a tale.

+++

I liked Billy immediately. I did not like his music. I have always had a difficult time following "rap", perhaps because my soul is out of sync with its jerky meter, but more so because it apparently must be played at stratospheric decibel levels to be acceptable by aficionados. I arrived home at the end of one exhausting day to find the flimsy plywood wall between us vibrating like the skin of a drum to Ice Tea or some-such, while Billy entertained his friends.

After polite hints failed, I finally pulled rank and ordered him to keep the thing turned down to a more neighborly level.

"Man, rap played low's like kissin' yo sister, sir", he protested.

I replied, "But we have to share a very small area. How'd you feel if I played Italian opera that loud?" He made a face and nodded. I explained how loud music can damage his hearing. As he rolled his eyes, I mentioned Grieg, Beethoven, and Tchaikovsky as examples to support my argument that music did not have to be loud to be powerful. However, in the end, I knew that this meant nothing to a kid who thought Opus was a character on "Mayberry RFD". It was enough that he agreed that his freedom to enjoy his music as he pleased ended at the door of my cubicle. We compromised on a blaster setting slightly below "stun" that created only a muted rumble through the adjoining wall, and I went back to my nightly reading.

+++

I noticed one day that I had not heard any music at all from Billy's hooch for some time. The silence was blissful, almost too much so. As much as I hated to admit it, Billy's (subdued) rap had become part of the ambient backdrop against which the days flowed. As he ladled peas and spuds onto my tray in the mess tent that night, I asked him why.

"Batteries're dead, sir, and I got no spares", he shrugged, and of course since the generator produced 220 volt current, he was out of commission.

Against my better judgment, that night after chow I knocked on his door. "Here", I said, handing him a fresh unopened battery-pack from my supply. "Just keep it down, like we agreed".

Billy's smile positively lit up the room and he bobbed and strutted like the consummate dancer he was. "Yo, SIR!".

+++

Billy was true to his word, and we coexisted peacefully from then on. Our paths may never cross again, and I still don't like rap music. But it was Billy who carried in a bowl of hot soup from the mess tent when, days later, I was too curled up with cramps and diarrhea to move. I waved it away with a groan, but he placed the steaming bowl under my nose and ad-libbed (as I wrote it down later):

"Now, I ain't yo momma, Commandah Steve, (clap)

An' I ain't got no gold-stripe sleeve, (clap)

But 'til you suck up this-here stew, (clap)

Gonna stay right here an' rap on you," (clap)

Rap on you, (clap)

Rap on you, (clap)

'Til you do!" (clap)

When I could stop laughing, I croaked, "Anything but that" and took the bowl from his hands.

What's Left of Somali Air Force

Me and my Med Sky Skipper

Somalia Letters ...
"Dear Friends"

Demonstrating my Boy Scout knot-tying skill

01 Mar 1994

Ah, March is here at last in Somalia. Heralding the approach of the vernal equinox are the season's early and tender young thorns just appearing on the pando-pando scrub, and The First Buzzard of Spring in spirited competition with the natives for the freshest road-kill. **Operation Continue Hope** is entering the final phase, as we retreat in perfect order before an enemy who is advancing in utter confusion.

This week's selection of vignettes includes a glimpse of the folks in charge, and a lesson in foreign fixtures....

The Generals

Every good military operation needs at least one General, to shoot in case things get screwed up. In the case of Operation Continue Hope, we have at least three on hand, plus several-odd who keep flying in from Washington or Camp Swampy or wherever so they can claim to have served in Somalia for at least a day, which is enough to qualify them for combat pay for that entire month (your tax dollars at work).

The selection process for General is one of life's unsolved mysteries. I am certain there are lofty written criteria, and much cut-throat competition and selection boards and all, but in the end I think the Bull Elephants just gather in some smoky back room and draw names from a hat, discarding only those that say "Donald Duck" or some-such. Anyway, our three Generals are probably a fair sample of the range of basic types available. To protect their identities, and my career, I will refer to them as Doc, Sleepy, and Grumpy (the rest of the Seven Dwarves are assigned to Bosnia or Texas)...

+++

Doc is easily the best General we have. He is ruggedly handsome and has a disarmingly aw-shucks Gary Cooper manner. The thing I most admire about Doc is that he places much greater importance on substance than on form. If it works, don't fix it; if it's broke, he is concerned less with whom to blame than how to make it right. One would think this approach to management mere common sense, but it is depressingly rare. I will remember Doc most for his humanity, and sense that his genuine concern was more for our well-being than for numbers on a chart describing our status in this hell-hole. An old girl friend of mine (the crazy one that was into tarot cards and incense) would have said that he "exuded positive karmic energy".

His was one of the fortunate draws from the hat. More than that, he is the kind of leader that people willingly follow into harm's way.

+++

Sleepy likes his creature comforts, and does his Generaling from a custom padded swivel rocker that looks as incongruous here as a gold plated putter. It is not enough for Sleepy to be fed information via verbal report or even memo; he wants everything presented daily on a series of overhead transparencies at formal briefings. His preference has resulted in a thriving cottage industry devoted to the production of charts, graphs, and bulletized statements on these "slides". Since everyone here wants to please Sleepy and thus earn the merit badges vital to promotion, every officer tries to outdo the other in the beauty and intricacy of their slides. It comes down to this: skill at Harvard Graphics translates into credibility and worthiness. The more inscrutably impressive and pictorially baroque the slide, the more weight that officer's report has and the more convoluted the subsequent discussion and analysis. One hapless Army major, when his project was completed and he therefore had no slide to present, began casting desperately about for any new topic to brief to Sleepy. If he did not, he would be sent home, and he had not been here long enough to earn the requisite merit badges. He finally found some trivia expandable to four more weeks' worth of slides for Sleepy, and was thus redeemed. I am convinced, after being both witness and party to this charade, that US forces would be out of Somalia in 72 hours if the paper supply were to run out or the overhead projector burn up.

+++

Grumpy earns his name and reputation by striking fear into the hearts of all lesser beings in his vicinity. He was also my reporting senior. He is a brand-new General and therefore must establish himself as A Force to Be Reckoned With. I have seen Grumpy's ilk before, in the playgrounds of forgotten little schools and the back alleys of hardscrabble factory towns: pugnacious bullies who delight in the misery they inflict on others, in their ignorance equating instilled fear with the recognition for which they are so pathetically desperate. Grumpy doesn't want slides, thank God.

His pleasure is to line everyone up in a room and single out one or two individuals to whom he will fire multiple questions on everything under the sun. Almost always, there will finally be one the victim cannot answer, then Grumpy verbally beats up and abuses him without mercy in front the group. I have only once been his Target du Jour, and managed to spoil the game by using Navy concepts and terminology, an area about which he has even less knowledge than he does of human nature. Grumpy was finally humbled in a small unexpected way when, engrossed in a particularly vicious harangue, his upper dental plate came loose and spewed forth in a graceful arc, spinning to rest on the floor. Since to replace it in his mouth without disinfecting was to invite any number of dire Somalian illnesses, the last part of his lecture came out, "Phoob bi bake byselb gleer?" and lost much of its effect. May the fleas of 1,000 camels infest his nasal hair.

Puzzles in Porcelain

The Mediterranean Sky is an aging Greek passenger ship which the Navy has contracted to ferry our troops down to Mombasa from Mogadishu. We can't fly everyone directly out from Mog because Aidid could hold a pigeon shoot & give us a better reason to waste him than we can use now. I had the task of escorting the first group of soldiers through the ship, familiarizing them with basic concepts like port/starboard and forward/aft. This group would then pass their newly-acquired nautical savvy on to the rest of the Army folks as they came aboard. Most of these troops had never set foot on a ship of any size before, let alone on a passenger liner. The Med Sky's elegance is somewhat faded by her years, but she boasts the genteel sophistication of traditional European luxury: walnut paneling, parquet floors, brass fittings and fixtures, plush carpeting, etc. I led my wide-eyed Army entourage through one of the first-class staterooms, pointing out the various features. One sergeant with a pronounced Texas drawl seemed fascinated by the bathroom bidet, and he was still fiddling with it when the rest of us walked forward to the dining areas. An hour or so later I mustered the group at the gangway and fielded several questions & comments.

As the rest of the group filed off, the Texas sergeant hung back. "Gotta admit, sir, ah am for sure impressed. Them Greeks'r real clever fellas", he said, shaking his head in wonder.

"How's that, Sarge?", I asked. "Hell, ah ain't never seen such fancy gadgets, even in the states. Them drinkin' fountains next to the john are a great idea. 'Course, had to hunker down to reach it, but that don't matter none." I just didn't have the heart to tell him.

The Fly Decathlon

The vast majority of personnel here are just biding time, waiting for those of us (allegedly) in charge to tell them when to go home. Like in any large and idle group, folks invent various diversions to pass the time. One of the more unique is the Fly Decathlon. In the order of performance, the events of this three-day extravaganza are:

(1) **Iron Man Shoofly** - keeping flies from alighting on four open MREs at once. Contestants start wit:n 100 points and lose 1 point for each fly that manages to land. Blowing & scooping are illegal procedure.

(2) **One-Hand Swatting** - 1 pt for each fly taken with standard Swatter.

(3) **Two-Hand Swatting** - same rules as above, but with Mini-Swatter.

(4) **Freehand Snatchoff** - 1 pt for each fly taken with bare hands; this event is held with day-old garbage as bait. Serious contenders train for this event by saluting for weeks with 5-lb wrist weights.

(5) **Speed Sexing** - sorting dead flies by sex with only tweezers and magnifying glass. Requires tremendous knowledge and concentration. Tryouts eliminate all but the most ardent sports enthusiasts.

(6) **Stacking Competition** - piling as many flies as possible one on top of the other. This event puts a premium on engineering skills & in-depth savvy of the adhesive qualities of various wing surfaces.

(7) **Big Foot Tug-of-War** - adult bull Matabele flies, known for their great size and foul temper, are specially selected and trained for this breathtaking spectacle. Legs and wings fly as the two mighty bulls, harnessed together with dental floss, struggle in opposite directions until only one is victorious. Not for the faint-hearted.

(8) **Fleet Skeet** - as many flies as possible are taken with pea-shooter on the wing from a fixed blind. Once hit, a fly must stay down for at least 10 seconds for shot to count. Added element of excitement comes from the fact that some species charge the spectators when wounded.

(9) **Name That Drone** - the blindfolded contestants' knowledge of fly lore is put this ultimate test as they must identify spe-

cies, gender, and even age by merely listening to the sounds of their passage.

(10) **Fly Endurance** - possibly the toughest event of all. After smearing the contestant's face with a mixture of peanut butter and ketchup, a sandbag is tied over his head and 100 assorted flies let loose into the bag. The record stands at 1 minute, 42 seconds. The champion had to be sedated right afterward, and hasn't been quite the same since.

Wonder Women

I have referred briefly in my letters to the female contingent here in Somalia, but perhaps have not adequately conveyed their special struggles. In many ways, they have it rougher than the men, living and working as they do in (what was until recent political changes) a "Man's World". Many old myths have died hard here, not the least of which is the Ozzie-and-Harriet notion of Gender Division of Labor.

With the exception of greater upper body strength, the men have no job-related advantages. To the contrary, mil-

My Somali office staff

itary females in Somalia have fewer and poorer sanitary facilities, longer walks home to their quarters, and a greater burden of proof that they can Do The Job.

My favorite lady here was Adelle, a pretty, blue-eyed, middle-aged mother of three whose joy is riding Harley's with her retired hubby back in Oklahoma. Adelle's day as

Mi-Wei, my administrative assistant

Army Chief Warrant Officer at the port is more demanding than what most stateside folks do in a week. She is Hollywood's model Frontier Mom: a mixture of strength, ingenuity and tenderness, equally able to bake a pie or shoot Injuns from horseback. We met while waiting for a ship to dock, and I saw her diminutive 5'4" uniform and hardhat walking the pier. I was there to meet the ship; she was there in charge of a gang of stevedores to load it. We shared cold MREs, talked about our separate lives, and became friends. Adelle and I eventually worked four ships together, and as a veteran of nearly thirty years in this business I had not seen a better crew chief—and told her so. One day she looked at me strangely for a long time, then asked me why I wasn't married. Had been twice, I told her, and was still shopping for number three. The inflection of her question made it a compliment, and some quiet electricity passed between us that said: another time, another place, another life, and you and I could have done well together. We shared a tearful hug when she left, two ships that passed in the night and paused, ever so briefly, just long enough to say goodbye.

Lemonade Dreams

My sub-conscious mind plays its oldest movies here. Perhaps it's the unyielding Army cot, or the texture of African air, but my dreams include a procession of plots and images that I had thought

My office in Mogadishu, 108 degrees

were forever relegated to the attic of memory. One recent re-run is the scene in Lawrence of Arabia when Peter O'Toole staggers into the officers' club in his dusty, tattered Arab garb, (remember?) having crossed the desert on foot. He rasps one word to the bartender: "Lemonade", and is clearly ready to cut the man's throat to get it. Sort of the way I have felt some days. In other dreams, I have chewed out a roomful of Generals for the stupid, sandbox games they play. In yet another, I am again a young sailor on the bow of my first ship, bound for a red sunset over distant Vietnam as Bob Dylan wails in concert. But the dream that I was most reluctant to quit, pulling the cover over my head even as the alarm rang, was the one in which I stepped off the plane and saw you there—all of you. Whether you know it or not, you have sustained me through this trial.

Part of a warrior's will to survive and overcome is the knowledge that he does so for the sake of brothers, sisters, friends, and family far away.

You were all waiting for me, standing at the bar, when I asked for Lemonade.

+++

Somalia Letters ...
"Waa Nabad!"

Damage to the Pier

10 Mar 1994

This will be the last of my letters from Somalia. "Come Saturday Morning, I'm Going Away With My Friends" on a medevac C-141 to Germany via Cairo, then London in time for high tea on Sunday...

(THEY'RE COMING TO TAKE ME AWAY, HA-HA, HO-HO, HEE-HEE!!)

....in front of a crackling fire at the Tudor Lodge. I look around me now & see an alien landscape, where the geometry and gentility of "civilized" rules do not apply.

At some point, words utterly fail. Words cannot begin to convey the stark hopelessness and cruelty of this place, or the acrid smell of fear from thousands of innocents, or how it could be that the very same sun broiling Mogadishu at this moment clears the morning mists on some golf course in Little Rock. Nevertheless, Somalia has been my home for many weeks, now. I will not miss leaving. I WILL miss the wonderful friendships I have made, forged from the bonds of shared adversity, and remember all my life the fundamental lessons taught here: Gratitude and Appreciation.

So here, my friends, are the last of my on-scene impressions.....

Feral Cats

I first noticed the feral cats as quick black shadows flitting across my peripheral vision, one night when the camp generator had quit and we hooch buddies were standing around in the dark. My best Wyatt Earp quickdraw was stopped halfway up by a Recon Master Sergeant: "Don't shoot, sir, it's just cats!" "Whaddaya mean 'cats'?", I whispered, nervously thumbing the safety back and forth on my pistol.

"The feral cats, sir. One-time house cats that went back wild, the way they were a million years ago. They won't bother us in a group like this."

I wasn't completely satisfied with this brief history, and determined to find out more about these feline ghosts. Further research in the following days revealed that, indeed, there was a thriving population of once-domestic cats that had been abandoned by their Somali owners and become, through successive generations, truly wild. Also LARGE. The first time I saw one clearly in the daylight, it more closely resembled a greyhound than a house cat: long and lanky, with a fox like snout and incredibly fast as it loped through the dune scrub behind the helo hanger. I also learned that they hunted in packs and were, in fact, known to attack and kill small children and elderly persons caught alone in the back country. Hunger made them bold, and I looked up from my books one night to find one staring in from atop the sandbags outside my window screen, his eyes yellow and luminous and very non-domestic. His daily problem was simple: kill or starve. Had his great-grandpa been a cuddly kitten lapping goat's milk from some laughing child's fingers? And what dark spirit drove him now?

"You do what you must to survive, don't you?", I thought at him. As if in answer, the feral cat yawned hugely, pink tongue curling between his sharp, white teeth, then he disappeared as smoothly as a puff of grey smoke. Will the Somalis, when the world turns out the lights, also evolve into a half-human version of their cats? I fear that these are just the shadows of a deeper, darker night to come....

ECHOES OF THE STORM

DEJA VU FOR BREAKFAST—FLASHBACK

The call comes in the middle of a rerun of African Queen. I am tempted to let the answering machine do its neat little screening number while I lose myself, for possibly the fiftieth time, in Bogey's irrepressible character. The pleasant fog of nostalgia that surrounds me when I see this movie is not something I wish to disturb. Alas, instinct tells me to pick up the receiver.

"Is this Commander McMikle?", asks the impersonal voice. Well, I know immediately that it's not someone selling time share condos or Bd McMahon telling me I've won a million dollars, so I answer, "Yes?".

"Sir, I'm calling to inform you that you are being activated

Me and XO LCDR Heim
Me and my Executive Officer, Lieutenant Commander Heim

The last ones board

effective 12 August 1990."

"Say again?" The layers of fog were burning off rapidly now.

"The MSC Commnader has directed me to inform you that you are being activated. You've been called up, sir."

"WHAT?" The dreaded words rang in my ears.

That simple exchange is to start me on a journey to the other side of the world, and to turn my life upside down. Saddam Hussein has crossed the border in Kuwait, and we are all on stand-by alert. Especially those of us who deal in sealift logistics, and ESPECIALLY (I remind myself) those of us who happen to have some command of Arabic.

BAHRAN — THE NIGHT OF THE HASH HOUSE HARRIERS

Only the British, with their delightfully wry wit, could have dreamed up a group like the Hash House Harriers. Where and how they originated, I haven't many clues. Someone told me that the Harriers were formed in Burma in WWII, and that there is a legendary Hash House Restaurant, like the equally legendary Brass Monkey, that is the namesake.

But the Harriers themselves are real enough. Being with them evokes all the images that we Americans have of the Brit Mystique: moustachioed stiff upper lips as the wogs charge in the desert, gin and tonics on the veranda, battered leather flying jackets with white silk scarves, and Pip-Pip Cheerio Old Boy.

The Harriers are basically a running club, evolved into a poor man's version of the classic British fox hunt. There are "Hares", young ladies bedecked with rabbit ears and cotton tail, that run out into the desert scrub and leave a trail for the "Hounds" (everybody else) to follow. The whole thing is designed to make everyone run in circles in the wilderness for several hours. When a Hound spots a trail marker, he calls "On, on!" to tell the others he has caught the scent. Because the cunning Hares often plant false trails and do other mischievous things, the calls of "On, on!" are many and constant.

All this running in the desert air gives one a truly prodigious thirst, which I suspect is the true purpose of the entire exercise. At sunset, the weary mob builds a bonfire, drowns itself in cold beer hauled to the spot by supporters, and begins the Ritual of the Great Hash House Mystery.

Steve Martin comes to boost moral

The "Dirty Dozen plus One"—my Desert Storm crew.

And here's where I come in. A good buddy of mine had asked me to come to a Monday night run several times, and finally I had no good excuse. "You'll need some good running shoes", he said, and helped me pick out some new Adidas at the American exchange. I was to learn some hard lessons from this purchase.

As long as I live I will never forget the sight I saw today. Walking down the hall, resplendent in full military battle dress and armed to the teeth, were two young Saudi soldiers. They were holding hands and grinning at each other like Cheshire cats. What a strange country this is, I think for the thousandth time: approach a woman in public and the *mutthaween* will throw you in jail and eat the key. But you can go shmooning with your boyfriend in front of Allah and the whole world without a second thought. These guys would be right at home in San Francisco.

I have noticed that the Saudi soldiers in general tend to fall into two basic body groups. First, you have your "Tubby" group, in which most men tend to have the general shape of a pear. This could explain the reason for the extra-heavy-duty belt loop sewn into the middle of the back of their uniform trousers: no matter how big the belly is, the butt tends to drop straight down, like Washington's nose at Mount Rushmore.

Then you have your "Barney Fife" group, which cast no shadows if they have the sun to one side. These poor souls resemble children wearing Daddy's war souvenirs. One does not get a warm fuzzy about their military prowess when it takes two of them to lug one machine gun. We in this country want our soldiers to be Ramboesque, with bulging muscles, ripped clothing, a rag tied around the head, and blood in the eye. These poor guys just don't fit the image.

TIME-WORN TRAILS

I was reminded today that we are not the first actors on this stage. In Bahrain, for instance, archaeological sites of the Delmon Culture date back 5,000 years. Locals insist that the tiny island is the original location of the Garden of Eden. (Yes, the Muslims believe in a Garden of Eden, along with the entire Adam-Eve-Serpent legend.)

There is a tree in roughly the middle of island called the Tree of Life. Traditionally, it is an absolute "must see" if you are going to Bahrain. Also traditional (so I found out) is the breakdown of the bus for at least two hours once it has arrived at the Tree. This is to allow the hordes of vendors, who happen to be relatives of the tour guide company owners, time to ply us with their brass pots, praye rugs, T-shirts, and other goodies manufactured in Taiwan.

"The Tree of Life" in Bahrain. Locals claim this was the Garden of Eden.

BONUS

ROAD BIRDS
I Have Known

<><><>

GOOD INTENTIONS, BAD SOLUTION

The 1973 Oil Embargo, imposed by the OPEC (i.e., Arab) nations as a geo-political economic strategy, created a short-term and artificially-induced oil shortage. Fuel shortages, long gas lines, and soaring gas prices were the result. America's response was the Emergency Highway Energy Conservation Act of 1974, signed into law by President Richard Nixon. This ill-conceived piece of legislation was a perfect example of the one-size-fits-all mindset of Big Government. At the ground level, what came to be known as the "Life Under the Double-Nickle" was imposed on American drivers. By imposing a universal 55-mph speed limit, the government hoped to reduce fuel consumption by forcing lower driving speeds. States were faced with losing all federal highway funding if they did not comply. This was greeted with almost universal disdain by the driving public, and an unofficial protest movement started almost immediately. The sale of everything from private radar detectors to defiant bumper stickers soared. For the two decades that it lasted, there was an entire counter-culture genre of songs, movies, and trivia that grew out of the public's disdain for the Double Nickle. Country-Western songs, like *"Convoy"*, *"Wolf Creek Pass"*, by C. W. McCall, *"Six Days on the Road"* by Dave Dudley, and movies like *Smokey and Bandit* with Burt Reynolds enjoyed great popularity. In Western states especially, where long, straight roads through barren landscapes were common, defiance of the Double Nickle became a pastime.

It was in this environment that I drafted the book, Under the Double-Nickle, in 1979. I created an entire flock of "RoadBirds" as a parody of the different types of drivers that populate America's highways and byways, and hired a professional, artist to depict them. The entire book never saw the light of day, but as I was writing Did I Ever Tell You?, I ran across my old manuscript and decided to include it as a humorous digestif. The biggest takeaway from that ill-fated legislation, for me at least, is that there are limits that Americans will accept on their personal freedom. Many consider some types of intrusion and restriction to be a direct assault on the liberty that we enjoy.

And to that, I will simply say: ROADBIRDS ROCK!

Enjoy...

WALTER'S TWITTY
(Hypertentia nervosus)

Appearance: Freshly scrubbed, well-groomed balding male, age 45-65. Usually wears glasses: cap or hat set squarely on head; expression of poorly controlled panic. Grips wheel tightly in both hands at precise 45° angles to horizon. Sits with shoulders planted on seat back and arms nearly straight.

Vehicle: American or Japanese sedan, solid blue, grey, white, or brown; painfully clean and polished. Factory standard hubcaps; minimum of optional features. Car interior equipped with four trash receptacles. May have toy dog with bouncing head in rear window deck, along with box of facial tissue.

Bumper Sticker: "AAA"; "Let Me Tell You About My Grandchildren"

Habits: Drives at 54.9 mph, precisely in center of right-hand lane. Usually accompanied by similar-age female, sitting as far away from driver as possible. Comes to complete halt at all stop signs. Makes turns without releasing two-handed grip on steering wheel. Signals turns three blocks in advance. Taps horn at birds, squirrels, and insects in roadway.

Recommended Tactics: Tailgate until subject becomes agitated, pulls to extreme right shoulder to allow you to pass.

Related Species: White-Faced Creeper; Yellow-Bellied Curbskimmer; Sniveling Quail

WALTER'S TWITTY

THE COMMON BOOBY
(Homo genericus automotilium)

Appearance: Adult males and females unremarkable to the eye. Garb and fixtures tend to be bland and passive in spite of great diversity. Males and females both display similar facial expressions (bored and boring).

Vehicle: American, Japanese, or German sedan or hatchback (Toyota station wagon seems to be a current favorite. Car colors tend to be lively and bright, contrasting vividly with occupants. (bored and boring).

Bumper Sticker: "I ❤ (Whatever)"; "My Other Car Is (Any)"; "(Name of Sports Team)"

Habits: Represented in far greater numbers than any other species, the Common Booby is found literally everywhere at all seasons. It is nocturnal as well as diurnal, although greatest activity noted is around 8am and 5pm on weekdays. Common Boobies reproduce at a tremendous rate (especially on weekends when TV selections are poor). Highway driving speed is generally 55-65 mph. Once in the passing lane, they display a great reluctance to actually pass another vehicle, seemingly preferring to ride side by side and inspect other cars' occupants at close range. Generally predictable and even-tempered, the Common Booby is easily enraged by another driver's failure to dim high-beam headlights at night.

Recommended Tactics: None. This species provides the environmental backdrop.

Related Species: Great North American Turkey; Bleary-Eyed Grouse; Ruffled Sapsucker

COMMON BOOBY

RUBBER-NECKED GANDER
(Touristogawker aggravatans))

Appearance: Adult male or female, age 45-70. Glasses, golf cap, or hat. Short-sleeved shirt of lurid design. Nearly always accompanied by one or more of opposite sex. Females invariably wear sweaters, regardless of outside temperature. Well-tanned, bland facial expressions.

Vehicle: Conservative late model sedan, usually of American manufacture. Out-of-state plates. Clean, well-maintained exterior. Rear of vehicle nearly drags pavement from weight in trunk. Profusion of tourist attraction stickers and decals cover windows and bumpers. CB antennae are commonly seen, as are parcels, suitcases, clothing, and a large variety of miscellaneous items piled high in seats and rear window deck. Visible souvenirs often include ridiculous straw hats covered with flowers and fruit, clay animals, and cheap paintings on black velvet.

Bumper Sticker: "Don't Push, I"m Pedaling As Fast As I Can"; "Disneyland" "Knott's Berry Farm"

Habits: Usually active in the summer and early fall, the Rubber-Necked Gander takes to the highways in great numbers on annual southern and western migrations. Average traveling speed is 55-60 mph. Rubbernecks seldom travel at night except on the Sunday before they're due to return to their nesting grounds. The Rubber-Necked Gander is named for its characteristic habit of constantly swiveling the head back and forth while pointing at objects outside the vehicle. This habit makes them a hazard, since it diverts attention from driving. The Rubberneck is especially difficult to deal with when encountered in the city, where they tend to proceed with extreme slowness, drive the wrong way down one-way streets, and make abrupt turns without signaling. They show a remarkable attraction for state capitol buildings, and flock there in great numbers each season. They collect spoons, plates, mugs, ashtrays and T-shirts bearing the names of places they have visited. Afoot, Rubbernecks mill about with a characteristic penguin-like shuffle, often looking up, wearing cameras and rubber-soled shoes.

Recommended Tactics: Rubbernecks are consistent and predictable drivers, and can be handled with little effort. On the highway, they tend to drive in the right-hand lane and make frequent rest stops, so passing is no problem. In the city, they are confused, paranoid, and insecure when honked at. Best city tactic is to lean on the horn for 5-10 seconds; Rubberneck will either slam on brakes or pull over in great haste (fearing that they have violated some local traffic ordinance), enabling you pass or evade.

Related Species: Common American Vanplover; Bifocalled Tangerino; Yellowstone Duck

THE RUBBER-NECKED GANDER

DOUBLE-BREASTED HOUSE PIGEON
(Condom condominium)

Appearance: Adult female, age 30-45 years. Dark glasses with large square frames, hair either tied back in kerchief or extremely unruly. Clothes disheveled. Facial expression is usually haggard, visible emotions ranging from frowning concentration to angry shouting. Often seen driving vehicle containing numerous young in various states of disarray, along with large panting dog. More often smokes than not.

Vehicle: American-made station wagon, circa 1973-1979, faded and dirty metallic green, blue, or rusty tan. Radio antenna missing and replaced by bent coat hanger. Vehicle windows difficult to see into or out of due to layers of dirt, sticky fingerprints, dried soft drinks, etc. Hub caps missing or dented. Large clouds of exhaust smoke hide movements. Tail light and turn signals broken and non-functional. Rear license plate often hangs by one corner.

Bumper Sticker: "Merry Kay Cosmetics"; Happiness is Being An Ammway Distributor"; "Family Home Evening"

Habits: Slow and unpredictable; travels in fast lane at 49 mph, refusing to yield to faster traffic. Windows tend to be open except in coldest weather. Species is very aggressive and has been known to snatch right-of-way, parking spots, and even place in drive-in bank teller line from under the beaks of other species. Tends to make turns with no warning or indication. When encountered afoot, the Housepigeon is irascible and belligerent; may attack without warning with large handbag and/or colorful invective. Roosts frequently in parking lots of laundromats, bowling alleys, and fast-food restaurants. Once per year (usually in late spring), mass migrations of the Housepigeon occur at car-washes, where they gather for annual cleaning and molting ritual.

Recommended Tactics: Toss up several empty aluminum soft-drink or beer cans from window. Housepigeon will abruptly pull onto shoulder of road, median, sidewalk, etc. and send one or two young out to retrieve them. This gives you ample opportunity to pass.

Related Species: Bronx Dowitcher; Mottled Peasant; Suburban Cormorant

THE DOUBLE-BREASTED HOUSEPIGEON

THE GREY CRESTED LADY BIRD
(Senilia undulatus)

Appearance: Adult female, age 60-80. Black or blue dress with pink and white blossoms. Eyes look through (not over) steering wheel; pillbox hat, hair grey and tied back into bun. Large dangling plastic bracelets and bead necklace; chin held high to facilitate seeing over dashboard. Determined, stubborn expression.

Vehicle: Clean but peeling and faded 1962 Nash Rambler, 1968 Buick Le Sabre, or 1969 Ford Fairlane. Minimum of decorations or accouterments. Balding tires with white walls. May have dried weeds and branches stuck to undercarriage.

Bumper Sticker: "Easy Does It"; "Enjoy Beautiful St. Petersburg"

Habits: Moves erratically; applies brake and accelerator at same time, producing a somewhat jerky motion. Never exceeds 27 mph except on highway, then will risk 45 mph for short periods of desperation. Makes sudden turns without signaling, especially left turns from right-hand lane. Waits at least 5 seconds after light changes before entering intersection. Relatively oblivious to other drivers (cannot see motorcycles at all), horns, flashing lights, sirens, road hazards, or school zones. Large numbers make local migrations to cafeterias on Sunday afternoons.

Recommended Tactics: Back off at least 500 feet, then choose an alternate route to your destination.

Related Species: White-Faced Creeper; Yellow-Bellied Curbskimmer; Sniveling Quail

GRAY CRESTED LADY BIRD

THE SPECKLED YAMAHAHA
(Rapidus nipponesei)

Appearance: From a distance, the Speckled Yamahaha can be easily mistaken for its cousin, the Black-Footed Thrasher. The similarities lessen dramatically when both species are examined at close range. Unlike the Thrasher, the Yamahaha often looks as if it just stepped out of a road fashion boutique. Custom leather and brass fittings, designer jeans, and Frey boots. Fur-trimmed jackets and $200 sunglasses are relatively common. Blue jeans if worn, will have knife-edge creases pressed in.

Vehicle: Late-model Japanese or German motorcycle, equipped with a multitude of factory options. Windscreens equipped with AM/FM stereo, wet bar, and even cable TV are not unknown. Small matching one-wheel trailers are seen, as are matched sidecars. All equipment is maintained in sparklingly immaculate condition.

Bumper Sticker: "Milk Drinkers Make Better Lovers"

Habits: Males and females tend to ride together. Species will almost always signal turns and maintain steady pace consistent with flow of other traffic. Normal cruising speed is 65-70 mph. Tends to flock under overpasses during rainstorms. Gregarious in summer, the Yamahaha can be seen in large flocks much the same as the Thrasher. The two species do not mix well, however, and violent territorial battles over choice roosting grounds have been reported. The Yamahaha is really only the molting stage of certain other automobile-using species, which hold in common the tendency to revert to two wheels when four become restrictive to their mating urges.

Recommended Tactics: This is generally a friendly species and deserves every consideration, When passing, don't crowd, and be aware of the effect of your wind-stream. If being passed, be kind and fluid—you may molt and mate yourself, someday!

Related Species: Black-Footed Thrasher; Candooda Goose; Goggle-Faced Whippoorwill

THE SPECKLED YAMAHAHA

THE GREATER FLAP-TAILED TRUCKER
(Velocidates collosus rubberduckii)

Appearance: Adult male, age 25-35 years(although females of same age range may be seen occasionally); may have 2-3 day growth of beard, ball cap. Casually dressed; species is difficult to see in motion due to high cruising altitude and vehicle characteristics. On the ground, species often resembles the Country Jay or Greater U-Holler (q.v.); dark circles under red eyes, tends to smoke and/or chew tobacco and related substances. Terminally addicted to coffee.

Vehicle: The most obvious distinguishing characteristic of the Greater FlapTail is his vehicle. Mack, Kenworth, Peterbilt, or Diamond Rea diesel tractor is common, with infinite variations in color, trim, and features. Large rubber flaps over tractor and trailer rear wheels. Sleeper compartment and CB radio are nearly universal. Found hauling trailers with great variety of decorations and labels, but confined to a few basic designs. The rectangular metal variety is most common. Rigs are massive in size, dwarfing those of all other species except the Trumpeting Busbird and related types.

Bumper Sticker: "This Vehicle Paid $62 Billion in Road Use Taxes Last Year"; "Wide Turns"; "Old Truckers Never Die, They Get A New Peterbilt"

Habits: Self-confident and assertive, the Flap-Tail is found in great numbers on major highways, with nearly equal density over the entire continent. Slow and ungainly during take-off, once underway the Flap-Tail cruises gracefully at speeds of 65-75 mph, slowing to 55 mph only when the danger of predators is acute, or when road conditions deteriorate. Active during both daytime and nighttime. Speeds will vary predictably in hilly terrain, when the Flap-Tail will often attain speeds of 75-85 mph on the downslope, in order to gain momentum for his next uphill stretch. They can sometimes be observed in large flocks (called "convoys") of from 3 to 20 or even more units, which they form for mutual protection from marauding Smokeys. (See "Road Predators" section). Flap-Tails pose some danger to other species because of their large size, especially when they spray rain or snow in passing other drivers, blinding them. They also show a distressing tendency to tailgate small vehicles at high speed. Generally, however, the Greater Flap-Tailed Trucker is a boon to the DoubleNickle Protester, providing excellent protection, surveillance, and even momentum assistance from their slipstream effects. In most cases, their movements should be followed and imitated, since they (like you) are interested in driving from point A to point B as expeditiously as possible. They roost in large numbers at cut-rate motels and feeding stations. The language of Flap-Tails is rich and colorful, and has been the subject of much study and imitation.

Recommended Tactics: Flap-Tails should be encouraged as road companions and used for cover and as early warning lookouts. Whether or not CB communications can be established, your movements and signals should display goodwill and courtesy. (See the section on Defensive Tactics for specific ways to use the Flap-Tail's presence to your advantage). Honks and waves will usually generate a friendly reply.

Related Species: Chrome-Fronted Puffin; Trumpeting Busbird; Winnebagell

GREATER FLAP-TAILED TRUCKER

THE BLONDTUFTED TITMOUSE
(Foxobimammarus gigantica)

Appearance: Female, age 17-29, hair light to dark blond. Highly developed and prominent pectoral muscles, easily visible from other vehicles, due to species' peculiar habit of leaning far back in seat to prevent catching pectorals in steering wheel. Languorous expression with mouth half-open, punctuated with occasional grins and winks. Wears tight-fitting sweater, top, or T-shirt.

Vehicle: Late model bright red or yellow mid-size or compact, either domestic or foreign, with racing stripes, custom hub caps, and other visible options. Clean and well-polished. Custom license plate with driver's name ("KRIS", "MIKKI", etc.) Loud rock music audible through window. Beads, feathers, amulets or other indistinguishable items suspended from rear-view mirror.

Bumper Sticker: "Honk If You're Horny"; "Save. The Whales"; "Jazzercise"

Habits: Smooth, confident driving pattern, tending to 60-70 mph on highway. Enjoys being observed while appearing not to notice attentions of other drivers. Shakes head and brushes hand through hair frequently, turning head to one side to do so. Drives with one hand on wheel. Often becomes aloof or distant when honked at or waved to. Often found in company with females of other species possessing less attractive plumage. Prone to have flat tires or engine trouble on well-traveled thoroughfares on Saturday afternoons.

Recommended Tactics: CAUTION!!!! This species can be extremely dangerous, causing accidents of varying severity due to other drivers' loss of eye contact with road obstacles. Best defense known is to concentrate on baseball scores, count waterspots on windshield, or hum the National Anthem until danger is past. Otherwise, entire journey may suffer re-prioritization and subsequent alteration.

Related Species: Valley Chickadee; Squealing Tern; Brown-Crested Strutter

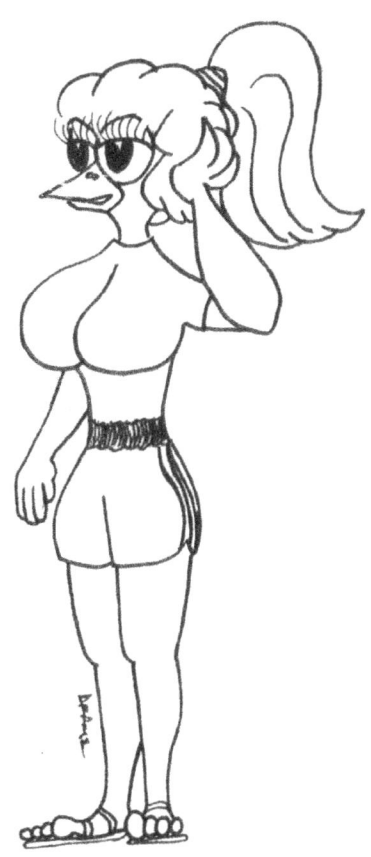

BLOND TUFTED TITMOUSE

THE MACHOCREEPER
(Lowmotilus molasses lacucuracha))

Appearance: The Machocreeper is one of the most colorful and distinctive species to be found in North America. Extravagantly dressed, meticulously groomed adult male, age 18-30. Mustache and/or goatee nearly universal; may have large-brimmed hat with elaborate hat-band, brim pulled low; wraparound dark glasses with cigarette dangling from side of mouth. Top of head or hat may be only portion of body visible. Chin tilted up, mouth closed in highly-practiced expression of disdain for rest of universe. Species may be difficult or impossible to observe due to smoked window glass.

Vehicle: Carefully restored and elaborately customized Pontiac Grand Prix, Buick Riviera, or Chevrolet Malibu, circa 1969-1979. Chassis modified to travel 3″ above pavement. Finish polished to a high gloss, upon which may appear elaborate pin-stripe designs. Diminutive steering wheel constructed of chromed chain links, chrome wheels with extra-wide tires. Large fuzzy dice, rubber skull, beads, feathers, or other species fetishes hanging from rear-view mirror. Plastic figurines on fake fur-covered dashboard. Smoked window glass; organ pipes and/or extra taillights in rear window deck. Horn plays Herb Alpert segments when operated.

Bumper Sticker: "I Brake for Blonds, Brunettes, and Redheads"; "Boycott California Lettuce"

Habits: Slowly cruises(20-25 mph) main thoroughfares and side streets of major cities. Meticulously careful to observe all traffic regulations. Preys on young females of own, or any other, species. Several Machocreepers often ride together in same vehicle for mutual assurance and support. Tends to frequent one-lane thoroughfares during peak traffic hours, when slows to 10-15 mph to conserve fuel. Apparently oblivious to the presence of other species. Can sometimes be seen performing dramatic puberty ritual with others of same species, wherein two vehicles bob up and down violently until one submits to the other.

Recommended Tactics: Do not sound horn or tailgate; this only induces the Machocreeper to drive more slowly. Remember that this species values his vehicle more than anything else. After determining that no law enforcement officers are present, simulate drunk driving mannerisms (weave, sing loudly off-key, assume idiotic expression and drool, etc.); Machocreeper will avoid and/or yield to you in order to protect his vehicle.

Related Species: Flat-topped Fonzie; California Candypiper; Rake's Rodbird

MACHOCREEPER

THE JIVE-BOTTOMED PECKERWOOD
(Honcus Honcus)

Appearance: : Carefully groomed adult male, age approximately 25-40 years. Extravagant plumage with tendency to unusual design and color, combinations. Cap or hat, dark glasses, personal stereo system. Facial expression is one of practiced nonchalance. Tends to favor necklaces, rings, and ear decorations. Exaggerated hand movements; tends to constantly touch face and hair. Wears horse curry comb in rear pants pocket for use in grooming rituals.

Vehicle: Late model Cadillac, Lincoln or Buick, frequently convertible, in white, black, turquoise blue, or lavender. All possible options. Finish and chrome polished to a high gloss. TV antenna, wet bar, CB radio, and customized spare tire compartment on rear of trunk may be present. Unidentifiable objects hanging from rear view mirror. Personalized license plate with unintelligible name or phrase, e.g., BUMP, NE1410S?, SKREEM, etc.

Bumper Sticker: "I May Be Slow, But I'm Ahead of You";"Leapfroggers International"; "See Beautiful Palm Springs"

Habits: Mainly found in warm, sunny climates, Peckerwoods are erratic and unpredictable in behavior. They often stop in the middle of traffic to communicate with others, comb their hair, or simply enjoy the view. Vain and arrogant, they seem to enjoy irritating other species and take great pains to position themselves where they can be easily seen. Highway speeds tend to be 45-55 mph. Peckerwoods are a gregarious species, and can be found roosting at expensive clubs and restaurants, where they call to one another in characteristically high, warbling chirps.

Recommended Tactics: Using a toy water pistol, spray a few rounds of water into the air over the Peckerwood. He will assume that it's raining and immediately pull over under the nearest shelter to avoid wetting vehicle and/or hairdo. For a more dramatic effect, substitute grape Kool-Aid for water; Peckerwood will think that his mascara is running and stop with great urgency.

Related Species: Giggling Swallowtail; Urban Soulfowl; Red-necked Loon

THE JIVE-BOTTOMED PECKERWOOD
(Honcus-honcus)

THE BLACK-FOOTED THRASHER
(Angelus satanicum)

Appearance: Belligerent and forbidding; hairy; sex and age are often difficult to determine. Black leather jacket and boots with levis are nearly universal attire, although vests may be sported in warm weather. Numerous cryptic and elaborate tattoos. Helmets of unusual design may or may not be worn, along with a wide assortment of ill-concealed and improvised weapons.

Vehicle: Customized Harley-Davidson, Triumph, or Indian motorcycle. Various chrome accessories and devices; double-decker seat, atrophied and arthritic-looking handlebars

Bumper Sticker: stylized marijuana leaf; "If You Value Your Life the Way I Value This Bike, DON'T F**K WITH IT".

Habits: Extremely dangerous and irritable when aroused, but can be suprisingly mild-mannered and affable. The Thrasher is often audible before he is visible. Species commonly travels in flocks of from three to twenty vehicles, and tends to be more active in warmer weather. The Thrasher follows an obvious but so far unpredictable migratory pattern, whole flocks converging on the same point at once from different directions. Feeds on copious quantities of beer and chili, which practice may also aid in propelling vehicle.

Recommended Tactics: Smile and make "peace" sign. Be absolutely certain not cut too close when vehicle or person may to crowd subject out of lane or passing; irreparable damage to you may result.

Related Species: Sooty Flycatcher; Speckled Yamahaha.

BLACK-FOOTED THRASHER

THE BLUEBREASTED STREET VULTURE
(Illegitimus copulator))

Appearance: Male or female, age 21-40; complexion ranges from ruddy to sallow grey. Sunglasses. Headgear can be octagonal or round military-style cap with shiny bill. Dark blue plumage with black leather appendages. Males tend to have spare-tire middles; females tend to resemble males. The species seldom smiles, and characteristically hooks thumbs in belt and cocks head to one side when on foot. Dark blue nylon jackets with imitation fur collars worn in cold weather, short sleeves with U.S. flag patches in warmer times. Bloodshot eyes are chronic and common.

Vehicle: Modified late-model Ford, Chevrolet, or Plymouth sedan pale blue, white, or black/white combinations. Steel and rubber push bars over grill. Commonly seen decal is "To Serve and To Protect" (obviously referring to fondness for tennis and athletic supporters). K-band radars preferred. Standard light bar; movable searchlights mounted next to driver's rear view mirror. Twelve-gauge shotgun in dash-mounted vertical rack. Species favors S&W .357 magnum or Colt .45 automatic. Clipmounted walkie-talkie on chest or shoulder. Shield-shaped badge with prominent number.

One-Liner: "Uwanna step outta da cah, pleeze?"

Habits: Street vultures infest the thoroughfares of cities large and small. They are under orders to produce revenue for their respective governments, and so select victims with an eye to the size of the probable fine involved. There are two distinct types, the Large-city and the Small-city. The latter is notoriously voracious and has a larger appetite for prey; the former seems more intent on simply surviving another shift in one piece. Large-city variety more often seen in pairs, moving constantly to cover large an area as possible, and tend to ignore minor violators in search of more exciting game. The Small-city Street Vulture is a crusader against crime, fighting off waves of boredom, swooping gleefully upon overtime parking violators and fleeing felons alike. Takes many victims by hiding in school zones during morning and evening hours. Small-city also tends to be more trigger-happy than Large-city, who is faster on the draw with a Miranda Warning Card than with a weapon. Females of both varieties are to be avoided, due to their large psychological appetites for Fear and Respect. If encountered, be sure to offer Fear and Respect in great quantities to avoid additional citations. (A little Groveling and Sniveling thrown in for good measure might even produce a wet smile and warning, instead!)

Recommended Tactics: If a Street Vulture swoops in your direction, look lost and confused. If it is your bad fortune to be captured, you must first determine clearly whether you are dealing with a Large or Small-City variety. If Large-City, you may employ impassioned pleas, arguments, and demented logic. Your best bet is the Good Story. The senses of the Large-City Street Vulture are so jaded that a really unique and ridiculous Good Story may cause him to release you out of gratitude for lightening his day. The Small-City variety is immune to these tactics, however, so a different approach is necessary. He must give up street for the ponderousness of the courtroom if you protest your citation, so produce your F. Lee Bailey Booster Club card and, using your best British accent, state your intention to defend your reputation all the way to the Supreme Court. (If a female of either variety has you, revert to Groveling and Sniveling).

Related Species: Wiggling Meterbird; Ghetto Snark.

BLUE-BREASTED STREET VULTURE

THE SPOON-BILLED TEENAGER
(Hedonistica agitans))

Appearance: Male or female, age 13-19 years. Personal stereo phones attached to ears. T-shirt with wide variety of sayings and logos. Blue Jeans, tennis shoes and windbreakers are nearly universal. Facial expressions range from stone apathy to rampant passion. Mouth nearly always open, has runny nose or other chronic cold symptoms.

Vehicle: Very wide variety has been reported, ranging from jalopy to limousine. No one reliably predictable make or model but must have high-capacity sound system for species to survive for any appreciable length of time. Feathered roach clip, garter, or graduation tassel suspended from rear-view mirror. Gregarious and active; drives aimlessly but at a respectable rate of speed. Communicates frequently with others of same species from behind the wheels of their vehicles, most often at stop lights and in drive-ins. Species is ingenious at finding hiding places after dark, frequents parks, beaches, and little-traveled areas. Has tendency to eject cigarette butts, cans, and other refuse from vehicle windows.

Bumper Sticker: "Things Go Better With Coke"; "Beautify America: Shoot A Redneck";"Support Your Local Sheriff"

Habits: Gregarious and active; drives aimlessly but at a respectable rate of speed. Communicates frequently with others of same species from behind the wheels of their vehicles, most often at stop lights and in drive-ins. Species is ingenious at finding hiding places after dark, frequents parks, beaches, and little-traveled areas. Has tendency to eject cigarette butts, cans, and other refuse from vehicle windows on Saturday afternoons.

Recommended Tactics: Pretend to be undercover narcotics agent. Point empty camera and/or binoculars at subject. He or she will hide face and avoid you with great alacrity.

Related Species: Clip-Handed Roachsnatcher; Snowy Ripsnorter; Whistling Puffswift.

THE SPOON-BILLED TEENAGER

THE KAMIKAZE CUCKOO
(Beepbeepians swooshii)

Appearance: Male, age 20-35 years. Car coat with collar turned up. May be chewing gum; leans forward with mouth slack and glazed facial expression. Other features difficult to see due to short time of observation.

Vehicle: Pontiac Trans-Am, Datsun 300X, or similar vehicle· will tend to be mud-spattered and dusty. Out-of-state plates.

Bumper Sticker: Radio station call letters

Habits: Appears extremely quickly in rear-view mirror, may be easily missed until right on your tail. Runs in fast lane when possible. Relative speed is normally 25-40 mph above that of other traffic. Utterly fearless and reckless, the Cuckoo demonstrates great skill and ingenuity in hitting puddles or snow patches in such a way as to blind other traffic in spray.

Recommended Tactics: (a) Pray; (b) Get the hell out of the way.

Related Species: Screaming Lowflyer; Texas Oilybird; Brazenwinged Bandit

THE KAMIKAZE CUCKOO

THE ORANGE-BANDED U-HOLLER
(Transientum elephantitum)

Appearance: Adult male, 21-40 years old, nearly always accompanied by female and one or more young. Casually dressed in jeans, sneakers, and T-shirt or sweatshirt. Male tends to drive bare-headed, wear black plastic sunglasses, chain smoke, need a shave, and wear a facial expression conveying resignation and/or expectant anxiety. Checks rear-view mirror constantly and slouches behind wheel. Mate often appears to stuffed and propped up in sitting position.

Vehicle: Overloaded, dirty orange, white and aluminum-colored truck with 16-26' box. Often seen towing small foreign car, Ford Pinto, or such on two wheels. Bicycles, dirt bikes, lawn chairs, and assorted paraphernalia strapped or wired to exterior of vehicle. Truck leans to one side. License plates on truck are never the same as those displayed on car.

Bumper Sticker: "Adventure in Moving"

Habits: The U-Holler is actually the migratory phase of any of a number of other species, and thus tends to drive according to the habits acquired in other, faster vehicles. This creates danger for himself and other roadbirds. The U-Holler, when encountered on the highway, is the picture of persistence. He travels in all weather conditions, night and day, and seldom stops for rest or refreshment. These strange and solitary creatures can be found in all regions, at any time of the year, and tend to drive much faster than their burdens would safely allow. The U-Holler normally cruises at 65-70 mph, causing his towed vehicle to sway violently. The carcasses of fallen U-Hollers are often seen on roadsides and on medians, victims of their attempts to cheat the laws of physics. They are almost never seen roosting together, but do frequent cut-rate gas stations during the same time periods.

Recommended Tactics: Following a U-Holler for too long is not advised, due to the danger of blowouts, tipping, loose gear, etc. If on a two-lane road, drop back until an opportunity exists to pass, then do so quickly. If on a divided highway, choose lane opposite and pass at maximum acceleration. U-Holler will always drive in the smoothest lane, regardless of which that may be.

Related Species: Trailing Weaverbird; Green-Backed Albatross

THE ORANGE BANDED U-HOLLER

THE COUNTRY JAY
(Apothecarium bovinus homunculus)

Appearance: Male, age 18-40 years. Checkered long sleeve western shirt, silk neck kerchief. Oversized western hat with feather or snakeskin hatband. Flared sideburns and/or droopy mustache. Passenger is usually similar-age female who appears to be riding in same seat as driver.

Vehicle: Late-model Ford, GMC, or Chevrolet pick-up truck, 4WD, with oversize tires and 60 square feet of chrome; gunrack in rear window; CB antenna; one or two large dogs in truckbed; fog lamps; Confederate flag occasionally seen on southern variety.

Bumper Sticker: "Cowboys Stay On Longer"; "Let's Rodeo"; "When Guns Are Outlawed Only Outlaws Will Have Guns"

Habits: Hat is nearly integral part of body (often not removable, judging from frequent wearing indoors at bars and restaurants); hat thus tends to restrict the flow of blood to brain, producing eccentric and erratic behavior. Guns engine in bursts of speed, then slows to near-crawl. Loud wailing noises (mourning rites?) audible from vehicle interior. Brown, wet globules frequently emerge from driver's window.

Recommended Tactics: Stare at hat, point and snicker. Country Jay will become apoplectic with rage, swallow tobacco, and pull off road to throw up. CAUTION: try to get as good a head start as possible.

Related Species: Brown Chipstomper; Old Crow; Daniel's Jackdaw

THE GREAT SWAGGERING COUNTYOWL
(Anus flammeus)

Appearance: Usually male, 30-45 years old. Slack expression, pot belly, broken veins in nose. Southern variety drools and chews snuff. Uniforms most often tan or green, sometimes tending to light blue. Moustaches and western-style hats are common, as are topped boots. Brown or black leather belts support a wide variety of accouterments ranging from mace canisters to pocket knives. Chrome-plated handcuffs, stylized handcuff or hangman's noose tie-tac, and various other decorations adorn uniform. Star-shaped badge in gold with blue letters. Shirt usually needs tucking.

Vehicle: The Countyowl usually operates within a limited budget, therefore the vehicle used is usually ill-kept and decrepit. Chevrolet and Ford sedans are universal, usually 2-4 years old and showing obvious signs of wear and tear. Green/white, black/white, and brown are favorite vehicle colors. Interior is likely to be littered with refuse and coated with cigarette tar. Light bar· simple "bubble" lights found in more rural counties. Older model hand-held K Band radars are popular, although wealthy counties may provide state-of-the-art gear. Species favors .45 caliber Colt automatic, although the Countyowl has been known to employ a tremendous variety of weaponry, including shotguns, hunting rifles, submachine guns, bazookas, flame throwers, and light field artillery. He is also more likely than other species to employ blackjacks, hunting knives, spiked bludgeons, and other medieval implements of persuasion.

One-Liner: "I'm gonna give ya a field sobriety test: close your eyes, put your fingers up your nose, and wiggle your left ear."

Habits: The Great Swaggering Countyowl literally enjoys a captive audience, and surrounds himself with all the trappings of machismo. He is a solitary, lonely hunter who is also an adrenaline addict. His happiness most approaches the orgasmic level when he finds justification to use lights and siren. He will often entertain captured prey for an especially long time, taking great pains to print his citation legibly. This habit is due in part to the necessity of producing twelve carbon sets, and in part due to the fact that spelling and grammar are not his strong suite. He loves to follow "suspicious-looking" vehicles until the driver nervously commits some minor transgression (touching white line, etc.), then performing thorough field investigation. His favorite prey is the "Dirt Bag". A "Dirt Bag" is any roadbird who (in the Countyowl's eyes) has too much hair, has a wise-ass expression, dresses like a city-slicker, drives a van with smoked windows, plays loud acid rock, or displays out-of-state plates from somewhere exotic like Oregon or Nevada. Countyowls are true creatures of habit; they like to lie in wait for prey behind obstructions, cruise slowly through trailer parks, and sneak up behind kids necking in the woods. They are fond of bean burritos, and spend long hours entertaining themselves by passing gas in creative, colorful ways.

GREAT SWAGGERING COUNTY OWL

Recommended Tactics: Countyowls are fascinated by armed conflict. If captured, present false ID card identifying yourself as an International Mercenary Commando Trooper, and explain that you are on the way to catch your flight to South Africa to help crush the guerrilla rebellion. He will breathlessly beg for details of your mission, forget to cite you, and may even offer to spring for a bean burrito just to hear your advice on the construction of jungle booby traps.

Related Species: Wattled Padpounder; Common Turnkee

THE BROADBANDED SPREADEAGLE
(Ursus fumosus terribilis)

Appearance: Usually male, age 21-45, blue eyes, short hair; deep suntan on left arm and left side of face. Campaign-style hat with leather hatband, dark glasses of military design. Side-striped trousers; crisp appearance overall. Penetrating expression resembling that of religious revivalist. Uniform is dark blue, green, brown, or combinations thereof. Large, shield-shaped badge with state logo.

Vehicle: Late model Ford or Chevrolet police-modified special. Immaculate condition. Black/white, white, or blue/white color combinations. Multiple antennae. Top-mounted light bar is common, but grill-mounted lights are seen often. Kustom Signals TR-6, MR-7, MR-9 X-band radars. Favored weapon is revolver in .357 magnum, wooden checkered grips.

One-Liner: "Would you mind restraining your dog, ma'am?"

Habits: The Spreadeagle is the most commonly encountered of road predators. He is the famous "smokey" of song, story, and epithet. They flock around the approaches to major population centers, and prey upon roadbirds entering or leaving the area. They are especially numerous near the inner borders of their respective states, and display a particular fondness for out-of-state victims. They have been reported, however, literally everywhere. A Spreadeagle is typically assigned to range over a large geographical area on one shift, but they prefer to take prey from a few favorite hiding places (overpass downramps are popular). They tend to remain stationary during peak traffic hours because of their tendency to collect long strings of other vehicles behind them as they drive. Most Spreadeagles will eventually do the decent thing and pull over after the line gets to be ½ mile or more in length. (Besides, it's distressing to have several hundred people radiating nasty thoughts at the back of your head). They are seen at all hours of the day and night, but are least active from 3am-7am weekdays, and most active during commuting hours and on holidays. Spreadeagles are relatively stable, straightforward, and predictable; due to the rigorous selection process that fledglings undergo, most of the ego-driven lunatic fringe sorts often found among the other predatory species are absent.

Recommended Tactics: Protesters should exercise the normal evasionary and deceptive tactics described in Chapter VI. Despite popular movies on the subject, you should never try to outrun a Spreadeagle; they enjoy a good chase more than anything else, and are notoriously persistent.
If taken by Spreadeagle, attempt to minimize the citation by expressing sorrow, disbelief at your speed, etc. Sometimes, an honest request for leniency will produce good results, as will humor. Avoid the confrontative approach.

Related Species: Shreiking Tailzapper

THE DOMEHEADED SPOKESMOKEY
(Birotundum puttputt)

Appearance: Adult male, 25-35 years old. Dark blue or tan uniform, riding pants with reinforced seat, black or brown leather jacket, white helmet, dark glasses or goggles, high kneeboots, leather gloves. All exposed skin tanned and peeling. Rugged, devil-may-care mannerisms and overall appearance. Smiles easily. Uniform and equipment in immaculate condition with knife-edge creases everywhere (including trouser fly). Expensive cologne fights losing battle with faint smell of gasoline. Oversized shield-shaped badge.

Vehicle: Full-dress white Harley-Davidson Electra-Glide with oversize rear compartment. All parts well-maintained and polished to a high gloss. Standard police decals and logos, diminutive red and blue emergency lights. Spokesmokies favor Smith & Wesson or Colt revolver in .357 magnum or .44 magnum caliber, wooden contour-molded grips with ribbed sights. Other equipment kept to minimum due to space and weight limitations.

One-Liner:

(Attractive female victim): "Hi, how are you today? In a hurry to be somewhere? I'm Officer Bill Smith, and I'd like to see your driver's license ...... thanks! Is this a current address, uh ... Sally?"

(Male victim): "Awright, you ..... pull it over!)

Habits: The Spokesmokey is the dashing, slashing man-o'-war of the roadways. He has all the panache of the World War I fighter pilot, lacking only a long white silk scarf to complete the image. Naturally egotistic and freedom-loving, the Spokesmokey loves to draw attention to himself and so stays in motion more than not. The thrill of straddling and controlling such a powerfully thrumming machine creates a sense of invincibility that flavors his entire outlook and personality. Spokesmokies usually hunt alone, although pairs are occasionally sighted. They dive on their prey in a breathtaking rush of speed. Older specimens tend to develop arthritis of the hip joints, along with chronic hemorrhoids, which make their outlook on life (and treatment of victims) less friendly than younger ones.

Recommended Tactics: If you are male, show great interest in motorcycle and related equipment. Ask questions related to its performance, mileage, cost, technical specifications, etc. Spokesmokey may show leniency and forget citation altogether while explaining his pride and joy. If you are female, run tongue-tip over half-parted lips, assume glassy-eyed expression, and caress fronts of thighs (your own). Whisper huskily, "My God, that's the most beautiful big white thing I've ever seen .... " Watch him preen, strut, and experience comic difficulty getting back onto his motorcycle.

Related Species: Spectacled Bustard

THE LAW MACAW
(Jurisprudens nauseam)

Appearance: Adult male, 27-45 years of age. Worn sports jacket and trousers, loafers, and tie decorated with various stains of mysterious origin. thick glasses contribute to a beady-eyed look; pasty, unhealthy complexion, but with flushed cheeks. Halitosis may be overpowering, due in part to dietary habits. Lean and hungry appearance overall. Bundles of pens, scraps of notepaper, and parking lot claim stubs protrude from pockets. Always seems to be in a hurry.

Vehicle and Equipment: Seldom encountered when behind the wheel, the Law Macaw does tend to favor conservative American sedans in beige, white, or dark grey. His driving habits are unremarkable (as is anything else about him).

One-Liner: "My client's rights in this matter ......"

Habits: The Law Macaw is a thoroughly disgusting creature. A shameless scavenger, he feeds upon the leavings of the major predators, sucking every last bit of substance from the bones of their victims. The Law Macaw is an expert at prolonging and complicating even the simplest event or action. He hovers around police stations, hospitals, and TV news rooms, where he spreads joy and goodwill among his fellow species by devising endless and ingenious schemes for litigation. Generally shunned by predators and roadbirds alike, the Law Macaw nevertheless fills a niche in society by providing an example of someone that even garbage collectors can look down on in revulsion and pity.

Recommended Tactics: Do not engage in conversation, answer any questions, or make any statements whatsoever. They can and will be used against you in any way possible. Never turn your back, even for a moment. Remove any debris from ground or floor around immediate area you occupy, to prevent the Law Macaw from falling and filing a personal injury suit. If approached closely, wave large crucifix and garlic strands.

Related Species: None that will admit it.

THE LAW MACAW
(Jurisprudens nauseum)

THE FUZZBUZZARD
(Gluteus aerocircitans)

Appearance: The Fuzzbuzzard is hardly ever seen by his victims. Reliable reports from the few who have seen one indicate that this elusive predator is usually an adult male, wears brown, tan, or blue coveralls with golf cap, and drinks profuse amounts of coffee. Little else is known about specific aspects of his appearance.

Vehicle and Equipment: Small single-engine aircraft OR two-place helicopter. May or may not have police markings.

Bumper Sticker: "Curse you, Red Baron!"

Habits: The Fuzzbuzzard patrols vast stretches of highway from the air, searching for fast-moving roadbirds. He seldom hunts roadbirds at night, but does patrol for victims afoot after dark in large cities. The Fuzzbuzzard cannot take prey himself, but serves as an alert and detection system for other predatory species, particularly the Broadbanded Spreadeagle. Fuzzbuzzards roost in dark bars between shifts, where they refresh and entertain themselves by composing unique graffiti on bathroom walls. These often contain a hidden message, an attempt to communicate sympathy and compassion with the roadbirds captured that day. He's, after all, himself a lover of speed.

Some examples:
Roses are red, violets are blue
I know you do it, 'cause I do it too ...

Arrive alive At 55;
You're looking great-Too bad you're late!

Recommended Tactics: Be watchful of the skies above you. Fuzzbuzzards detect prey by flying directly over a highway, so be suspicious of all small aircraft that exhibit that pattern. He will not remain in one area for long, so your best defense is to be as inconspicuous as possible until the danger passes. NOTE: Many states with limited budgets post signs that read: "Patrolled By Aircraft", when in fact they use few or none, (e.g., Wyoming, Arkansas). These same states place white painted silhouettes of planes on the roadway. The more such images you see, the more likely it is that the powers-that-be are bluffing, and the more unlikely it is that Fuzzbuzzards are a danger.

Related Species: Blue Chopperswift

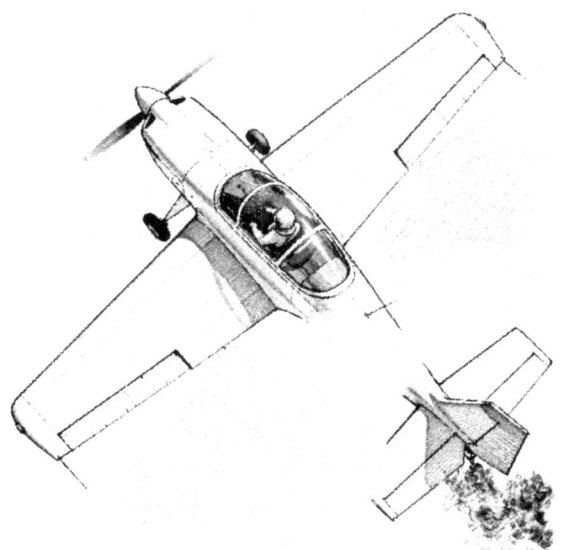

THE PLAIN BROWN GOTCHA HAWK
(Ursus fumosus terribilis)

Appearance: Wolf in sheep's clothing. Adult male 23-38 years old. Dark glasses with metal frames. May or may not wear uniform. Smugly professional manner with little wasted motion or effort. Non-uniformed types have overall appearance reminiscent of an insurance salesman. Uniformed variety will seldom wear headgear when hunting. Chews toothpicks and wears sardonic grin left over from the Spanish Inquisition.

Vehicle: Late model Ford, Chevrolet, or Plymouth sedan with no obvious police markings. Absence of whitewall tires combined with very plain hubcaps, is a dead giveaway. Colors ma; range among brown, white, or dark blue, but never pastel or two-tone. Singular lack of pinstriping, chrome, or other decorative bodywork lends a characteristically austere appearance to vehicle. Some varieties have searchlight mounted near outside rearview mirror, and this is always a sure sign of a Gotchahawk. Small CB antenna may or may not be evident. Lights and siren are mounted behind grill or carried inside the vehicle, therefore nearly undetectable. Wide variety of weaponry, tending to the James Bond variety.

One-Liner: "Do you believe in Murphy's Law?"

Habits: The Gotchahawk is easily the most feared of all road predators; he is just like Death itself in that he strikes with no warning. He appears when least expected, apparently out of nowhere, to shut down his startled and dismayed victims. His favorite prey is the Screaming Low Flyer, but he has been known to feed on all species, including the Trumpeting Busbird and the Greater Flaptailed Trucker. The Gotchahawk will often blend into traffic and rely upon his uninteresting appearance to deceive other roadbirds into driving the way they normally do (i.e., faster than the speed limit). In his spare time, the Gotchahawk enjoys ritually neutering small animals with a fork.

Recommended Tactics: Be cautious and prudent when encountering any vehicle matching the general description of a Gotchahawk. They are usually fairly easy to spot when in motion, and (as is the case with most road predators) prefer to prey on the high-rollers who drive 80+ mph. If, however, a Gotchahawk seizes you, try throwing up all over your clothes, driver's license, and registration. The Gotchahawk's fastidious sense of good sportsmanship (not to mention his dislike of puke-covered documents) will often be satisfied by this obvious demonstration of abject terror. Besides, his fun is over after he surprises you.

Related Species: Bentbeaked Roadblocker

PLAIN BROWN GOTCHAHAWK

About The Author

Commander Steve McMikle (Ret.), U.S. Navy

Dr. Steve McMikle, Cdr., USNR (Ret.), brings to these pages the hard-won wisdom of three decades in uniform, including combat deployments to Vietnam and the Persian Gulf, alongside years of scholarly work as a PhD and educator. Drawing on leadership forged under fire and refined in civilian life and the classroom, he offers readers a rare blend of operational insight, moral clarity, and practical guidance for navigating today's most demanding challenges.

With over three decades in the United States Navy, McMikle navigated war zones from Vietnam to the Persian Gulf and Somalia. He became a specialist in Muslim and African cultures, mastering the basics of languages like Arabic, French, German, Greek, and Swahili—skills that enabled him to build bridges in some of the world's most complex regions.

His combat credentials are matched by a decorated record of leadership and deep commitment to the men and women he served alongside. But what sets Commander McMikle apart is his unwavering curiosity and adaptability. After hanging up his uniform, he devoted himself to education, serving as a mentor with the Florida Department of Children & Families and as a state-certified instructor and martial arts expert, graduating over 700 students since 1977.

McMikle's expertise isn't confined to the military; he carries degrees in history, languages, sociology, and business, with further studies in education. He is a motivational speaker, platform instructor, and former deputy sheriff, embodying the rare blend of warrior, teacher, and public servant.

www.ingramcontent.com/pod-product-compliance
Lightning Source LLC
Chambersburg PA
CBHW070550160426
43199CB00014B/2445